STOKELY SPEAKS

STOKELY SPEAKS

FROM BLACK POWER TO PAN-AFRICANISM

STOKELY
CARMICHAEL
(KWAME TURE)

Lawrence Hill Books
Chicago

Library of Congress Cataloging-in-Publication Data
Is available from the Library of Congress

Cover photo: Stokely Carmichael speaking at a civil rights rally, 1970.
   Copyright Bettmann/CORBIS
Cover design: Sommers Design

This unabridged edition of *Stokely Speaks*, which was first
published in 1971, is reprinted by arrangement with the
estate of Kwame Ture

Published by Lawrence Hill Books
An imprint of Chicago Review Press Incorporated
814 North Franklin Street
Chicago, Illinois 60610
ISBN 978-1-55652-649-7

Printed in the United States of America

This book is dedicated to President Ahmed Sékou Touré and Mme. Touré and to my brothers and sisters in Guinea who have suffered much to maintain Africa's dignity and sustain Africa's will to survive.

Foreword

I don't know what I expected when I received and read this text of letters, articles, and speeches by the late Kwame Ture (née Stokely Carmichael).

The man wasn't a complete cipher.

During the period of my youthful membership in the Black Panther Party (Philadelphia chapter), this outspoken, fiery rebel held the rank of Honorary Prime Minister. When our West Philadelphia office held community political education (P.E.) classes, we often featured the Liberation Newsreel black and white film of the rally in the Bay Area for the freedom of Minister of Defense Huey P. Newton. There, standing tall, lean, and black as a Masai warrior, stood Stokely Carmichael, spitting fire and rage, lightly seasoned with his Trinidadian clip of the English tongue.

I had even met him, albeit briefly, in my life as a reporter, when I covered a speech he gave in the 1970s, in a run-down storefront in North Philadelphia. After the speech, he was gracious enough to grant a brief interview.

Yet, upon reading his own words, I was surprised. Indeed, I was surprised at how surprised I was.

For it dawned on me that, during my midteens, and even into my first fires of adulthood, I learned about Stokely by the words of others.

Press reports. It's amazing how those of us who consider ourselves revolutionaries still rely on the words of the white supremacist corporate press—a true enemy of the Black Liberation movement if ever there was one.

Or even in the Black revolutionary nationalist press, as, in my case, *The Black Panther*.

I was surprised, even though I'd read (long ago), and recently reread, *Black Power*, the work penned by him and Charles V. Hamilton.

I often wondered, in a critical, small-minded way, "How much of this was written by Stokely, and how much by Hamilton?" And while I'm sure I saw this book on shelves, on tables, and, yes, in recycling bins, I didn't buy it. I didn't read it. By then, the Party had declared him a "cultural nationalist"—a term that, at the time, was tantamount to Enemy. A good, loyal Party member didn't read such stuff. And, to my shame, I didn't.

I am blown away by his brilliance, his insights, his sharpness, his profound love of African people, and lastly, his humility.

In one of his last entries in this slim yet packed volume, Ture tells Black college students (at Morehouse and Federal City Colleges) that true revolutionaries must not bum-rush the mic but take the valuable time to study. He explains:

> Because revolutionary theories are based on historical analysis, one must study. One must understand one's history and one must make the correct historical analysis. At the correct moment you make your historical leap and carry the struggle forward. Not only that, you cannot rap if you really don't believe what you're saying, or if you don't know the answers. Fourteen months ago it became clear to me that the black community was heading for political chaos. *I knew that I didn't have the answers,* so it was silly for me to stay here and keep rapping about what I didn't know. Why should I stay here to get up on television and yell a lot of nonsense? It would only cause confusion in my community. I didn't want to do that. Confusion is the greatest enemy of revolution. (Italics added)

Boy—I bet you didn't see those kinds of admissions often among leaders! And speaking of leaders, what would history have been if Ture did not leave the Party? What if the Party was big enough, strong enough, mature enough to include his insights into their own? Ture writes (in "Pan-Africanism") of the "ideological issues" that separated him from the Party. Although he is not explicit, the issue was working with white radicals, something Ture found untenable. Ironically, the ideological positions between Huey P. Newton and Stokely Carmichael were perhaps closer than first thought. As early as 1971, Newton recognized that the Party's work with white radicals was unproductive, for "White radicals did not give us access to the White community because they do not guide the White community."[1] One cannot read Stokely's trenchant analysis of white liberalism without coming to the same conclusion (see his January 1969 speech, "The Pitfalls of Liberalism"). In the decades since this revolutionary era, we have seen how so-called radicals become liberals and, in current parlance, "neoliberals" (not to mention neoconservatives).

Moreover, one must be ever mindful of the efforts of the State to create, expand, and exploit divisions between Black revolutionaries. In perhaps the most infamous of the COINTELPRO documents yet uncovered, where the FBI announced as one of its primary objectives "to prevent the rise of a [Black] messiah," Stokely's name was listed among them.[2]

A steadfast Pan-African revolutionary, Ture worked tirelessly, almost literally to his last breath, to do the one thing that he repeated to every Black crowd he addressed: "You must organize. Organize. Organize!"

Perhaps his words, which reflect his brilliance, his courage, his ever-growing anticapitalist and anti-imperialist ideology, and his will to bring into being a Black revolutionary world, will feed a new generation who will heed his call.

—Mumia Abu-Jamal, author,
*We Want Freedom: A Life in the Black
Panther Party* and *Live from Death Row*
Spring 2006

---

[1] Hillard, David & Donald Weise, eds. *The Huey P. Newton Reader.* New York: Sven Stories, 2002.

[2] *See* FBI Memos: Feb. 29 and May 4, 1968. Churchill, Ward & Jim Vander Wall, *Agents of Repression: The FBI's Secret Wars Against the Black Panther Party and the American Indian Movement.* Boston: South End Press, 1988. 58.

Preface to the 2007 Edition

Forty years ago, on June 17, 1966—twelve days before his twenty-fifth birthday—Kwame Ture, then known as Stokely Carmichael, was catapulted by the masses of African people in Greenwood, Mississippi, onto the world's political stage when he reechoed their centuries-old demand for Black Power. It was at that fateful rally in Greenwood that Kwame deployed, for the first time before the world's media, the full range and power of his organizing capacity, his oratory and charisma. And thanks (no thanks) to the miscalculation of the United States government and media, a refreshingly new, young, black, and revolutionary voice and image was heard and seen for the first time, in every corner of the world.

That "Black Power Rally" boldly announced to the world, especially to African and oppressed youth, that a new generation had come of political age and had seized control of the world's political stage, even if only for one brief and shining moment. Kwame's words and demeanor, and the crowd's response to them and him, signified that a new wave of resistance, rebellion, and revolution had reached critical mass, and that it would take a radically different form. The effect was catalytic.

Five years later, in 1971, Random House published *Stokely Speaks: Black Power Back to Pan-Africanism*, thanks to the intervention of Toni Morrison, who had been Kwame's English professor at Howard University and was at the time an editor at the press, and to the editorship of Ethel Minor, Kwame's secretary and advisor in the Student Non-violent Coordinating Committee (SNCC), the Black Panther Party (BPP), the Democratic Party of Guinea (DPG), and the All-African People's Revolutionary Party (A-APRP). This seminal collection of Kwame's speeches and writings from 1965 to 1971 was published, according to Ethel, in order to document Kwame's "consistent growth and development as a revolutionary activist and theoretician." But, Ethel offered, "perhaps more important than summarizing the ideological history of a controversial black leader, this book also serves to some extent as the history of the 'Black Movement' during that [period]."

For six years—from 1965 when he founded the Lowndes County Freedom Organization in Alabama, the first Black Panther Party, to the publication of *Stokely Speaks* in 1971— Kwame, like the bold, "bad," black panther he symbolized, prowled the length and breadth of the United States and the world, wherever he was invited and permitted by hostile governments to visit.[1] He traveled a political path similar to and earned a place among other advocates of Pan-Africanism and socialism, including: Kwame Nkrumah, Ahmed Sekou Toure, and Mangaliso Robert Sobukwe; Shirley Graham and W.E.B. DuBois; George Padmore, C.L.R. James, and Claudia Jones; Marcus, Amy Ashwood, and Amy Jacques Garvey; Elijah Muhammad and Malcolm X; Ho Chi Minh, Kim il Sung, and Che Guevara; and a host of others.

Through experience and study, Kwame Ture came to understand that true freedom for African people is vested in self-reliance and self-determination, which is achievable only through appropriately scaled national unity. For him, that scale of national unity was continental and all-African. He believed, as Kwame Nkrumah correctly defined, that Pan-Africanism is

---

[1] From 1961, with his arrest and imprisonment during the Freedom Rides, to 1966, Kwame was arrested twenty-seven times. He was detained or arrested numerous other times between 1966 and 1985. When J. Edgar Hoover and the FBI launched COINTELPRO in August 1967, Kwame was its prime target. Also beginning in 1967, he was banned from traveling to or speaking in the British Commonwealth and French Community. He was also opposed by the Soviet Union, and the countries, movements, and organizations over which it exercised influence and control. His writings and speeches, especially Black Power, were banned, and their sales and distribution discouraged. The FBI, CIA, White House, and other governments received reports from the U.S. Embassy about his funeral.

the total liberation and unification of Africa under scientific socialism and that it is the only objective which, when achieved, will solve the problems that people of African descent face in every corner of the world. Kwame spent the last forty years of his life teaching about and organizing to achieve Pan-Africanism. It was through his oratory and organizing that Kwame made his greatest and most enduring public impact. Unknown, however, to most, he was one of the most prolific writers of his generation. Spanning more than three decades, his speeches, interviews, articles, correspondence, reports, memorandums, proposals, and other materials number in the thousands. Through *Stokely Speaks*, Ethel ensured the publication of the fifteen speeches and articles preserved in this little book that without her dedication would still remain in file cabinets and boxes, and on old reels of tape.

Thirty-five years after its initial publication, *Stokely Speaks* has been republished thanks to the unyielding work of Mrs. Mabel Carmichael, Kwame's mother; Nagib Malik, his sister; Lawrence Hill Books and Yuval Taylor, its senior editor; Michael Thelwell, the coauthor with Kwame of *Ready for Revolution: The Life and Times of Stokely Carmichael (Kwame Ture)*, who introduced us to Yuval; and the unyielding efforts of the A-APRP. Due to production considerations, the name Stokely Carmichael continues to be used instead of Kwame Ture.

I met Kwame in the summer of 1966 when he came to Chicago to help found the Organizing Committee for Black Power, speak at the University of Chicago, and attend the Nation of Islam's Saviors Day Program at the invitation of the Honorable Elijah Muhammad. From 1967 to his transition in 1998, I had the honor and privilege to work, study, and struggle with him in SNCC, the Illinois Chapter of the BPP, the A-APRP, the PDG, and a host of other organizations, movements, programs, and events. I currently have the honor and privilege to serve, with Nagib Malik as codirector of the Kwame Ture Work-Study Institute and Library, which is based in Conakry, Guinea.

I am honored and privileged to continue the work that Ethel began. I am also honored and privileged to share the responsibility of relaunching this classic with Mumia Abu-Jamal. His humility and honesty, as displayed in his foreword, is refreshing and was entirely expected. I also thank Pam Afrika for helping us make contact with Mumia, and Dr. Will Jones for his encouragement and editorial advice. Much respect!

Stokely Speaks is a time capsule, a blast from the past. It is also an educational tool, an organizational weapon for the future. It will enable and empower a new generation of youth and scholars, activists and organizers to begin to know and understand Kwame Ture as a man of thought and action, of work and study, of organization and struggle. It also affords an opportunity to intensify the struggle to challenge the historical and continuing efforts to "white" Kwame out of the history of the Civil Rights, Black Power, and Pan-African Movements, and to correct the myths, distortions, and deformations which encumber our understanding of him, his contributions, and his achievements. We hope that additional volumes of his speeches and writings will be published that document his continuing and consistent growth and development from 1971 to his transition in Conakry, Guinea, on November 15, 1998.

This book is Kwame's gift to African and oppressed youth worldwide. We hope they will read and study it, and that it will inspire, enable, and empower them to accomplish their historic task, as so many similar books inspired, enabled, and empowered Kwame and his generation to accomplish theirs. Who knows? Perhaps the new Kwame Ture, among our daughters and sons, granddaughters and grandsons, already exists, waiting for that historical moment when he or she too will be called upon to make a contribution to the forward march of progress and history. We trust that they will be "Ready for the Revolution!" whenever and wherever they are called.

—Bob Brown
Codirector, Kwame Ture Work-Study Institute and
Library Organizer, All-African People's Revolutionary Party
Conakry, Guinea, and Washington, DC
June 5, 2006

Editor's Preface

"This is one reason Africa has such importance: the reality of black men ruling their own nations gives blacks elsewhere a sense of possibility, of power, which they do not now have." The preceding quote comes not from one of Stokley's Carmichael's recent speeches but from "Power and Racism," the third chapter of this anthology. It was written in 1966, after the famous Meredith Mississippi March which had thrust the personality of Stokely Carmichael and the concept of Black Power into the lives of black people across the United States. I call these few words concerning the importance of Africa and the date to the reader's attention because they illustrate very well the central point which this editor wishes to focus upon: that this new collection of Carmichael's articles and speeches documents his consistent growth and development as a revolutionary activist and theoretician from 1965 until the present, 1971. Beginning with the first chapter, "Who Is Qualified?" through the final chapter, "From Black Power Back to Pan-Africanism," the speeches, in chronological order, clearly demonstrate the ideological development of the author—who has become one of the most loved, hated, respected, feared and misunderstood black men of our generation.

But perhaps more important than summarizing the ideological history of a controversial black leader, this book also serves to some extent as a history of the "Black Movement," during the past six years. For the concepts which Stokely developed during these years grew out of the collective experience of his study, travel and work. The work included: organizing for and working within the Student Nonviolent Coordinating Committee (SNCC) and later the Black Panther Party; founding and working with many other local and national black political institutions in the ghettos of the United

States; and speaking before his brothers and sisters whenever and wherever possible, trying to develop the correct political perspective and consciousness among our people. In acquiring this experience it is obvious that interactions with other co-workers, long hours of planning strategy and exchange of ideas, along with the hard lessons which America teaches those who dare challenge her methods of operating, have all helped produce Stokely Carmichael. His own growth and development cannot be seen in strict isolation from that of the movement, which in our generation started with civil rights, moved on to Black Power, and is now beginning to recognize and understand Brother Malcolm's call for us to internationalize our struggle and look home toward Mother Africa. Thus, this volume is of double importance to students of history and politics, and to all those brothers and sisters who profess an interest in the black liberation struggle, whether as activists or supporters. Although six years are but a dot on the historical spectrum, persons of African decent must surely admit that the past five or ten years have represented one of the most important and dynamic periods in our long struggle for freedom which began on the slave ships.

But, just as Stokely Carmichael is a product of this recent period of struggle, so has he also become one of the few men who can and does give meaningful, serious direction to our efforts. Having worked with Stokey Carmichael since 1966 and having been a close observer of his development into a national, then international leader, it is a most difficult task for me to jot down my impressions, observations and analysis, knowing that their objectivity will surely be questioned by many. But no one will deny the fact that black people living in the United States rejoiced at the appearance of the Black and Beautiful charismatic Stokely in 1966, which filled the vacuum left by Malcolm's death. How could we ever count the number of brothers and sisters who flooded the SNCC offices with requests for Carmichael to come to their schools, cities, towns, counties and organizations to speak, bring the message to them and help them organize?

Blacks here in America, and elsewhere by then, followed closely his 1967 travels in Africa and the Third World—some with pride, others puzzled, but all anxious to hear what he had learned and how it related to them. Upon his return, Panther leaders beseeched him to speak on behalf of the recently imprisoned Huey P. Newton, asserting that only he had the stature, influence and ability to help them publicize Huey's plight. Stokely's willingness to do this resulted in the party's declaring him Prime Minister of the Black Panther Party and of Colonized Afro-America in February 1968.

Shortly thereafter began a period of deliberate withdrawal from the public eye in which the author accepted only limited speaking engagements and concentrated his efforts on building the Black United Front in Washington, D.C., which he hoped would later serve as a model to be repeated in other cities and towns of America. At the same time, Stokely was quietly making plans for his future residence in Guinea, West Africa, having become convinced of the need for further study and of the need for us to establish concrete ties with the Mother Continent. The groundwork for these plans had been established during his 1967 visits with certain African heads of state and with Osaygefo, Dr. Kwame Nkrumah.

It was also in early 1968 that the American press began a clever campaign of attacks on Stokely Carmichael—all designed to discredit him on both personal and political levels. That these attacks and insinuations were deliberate fabrication was rarely even investigated or questioned by the "Negro" news media—they just dutifully repeated and reprinted the rumors white folks had dropped for them. Stokley's refusal to dignify the rumors by refuting them was interpreted by so many of our misinformed brothers and sisters as confirmation of the rumors.

Along with the well-organized anti-Stokely campaign in the mass media came attacks from within the black community from Panther leaders and other so-called Marxists, who began labeling him and all others who didn't follow the "party line" as "pork chop nationalists," "cultural nationalists," etc. It is to Mr. Carmichael's credit that he refused to dignify these "charges" and attacks—and further, to engage in personal attacks on the opposition. A little later, a few remaining members of the once dynamic and influential SNCC decided to "expel" Stokely, using certain "charges" as justification for the "expulsion." Once again, Stokely did not attack his adversaries on the petty, personal level, but preferred to debate the political issues—which are what the "expulsion" and all the name calling were really about. By this time it became clear that a whole lot of folks, from the government through the neo-Marxists to Black Power pimps in the ghetto, feared both Brother Carmichael's political ideology, and his personality which so forcefully presented that ideology.

Stokely remained silent, receiving insults from many who had idolized him only a few years before, from many who had received their early lessons in black consciousness from him, from many who had benefited by their association with him, and from those who had used his name and personality to help build their own thing. In January 1969 he left the United States for Africa, amidst further rumors and accusations that he was "running away" and "going into exile." The situation was very similar to that surrounding Brother Malcolm's departure for Africa in 1964, when so many of his close associates and co-workers began to accuse him of "going away when we need him most over here." During those hot summer months of the 1964 Harlem rebellion, while working as secretary in the Organization of Afro-American Unity (O.A.A.U.) office, I remember very well that some of our brothers and sisters even accused Malcolm of "being just another bourgeois nigger" (referring to his visits with African heads of states), while others could see no benefit whatsoever in his going to Africa. "What does that have to do with us when Harlem is on fire over here?" they questioned. Of course, very few would now want to admit their earlier lack of vision and understanding of Malcolm's mission.

Although Brother Stokely has sent a few messages back to our people in North America and although he returned for a few months in 1970, many have either not heard about the work he is doing in Africa or still do not fully understand its implications. Recently a sister asked me if Stokely "had gone over to Africa and found another cause." To this sister, to so many of our people who are confused and to the student of politics and history, I advise that you read this volume carefully, from beginning to end. Each speech demonstrates the logical growth and development which carried Stokely Carmichael from the Mississippi Delta to Conakry, Guinea. But, perhaps what will strike the reader most is the fact that certain revolutionary positions and ideas which Stokely holds today were also held by him several years ago—they have only been altered or strengthened by the passing years.

For instance, the reader will learn that Stokely has clearly always been anti-capitalist and anti-imperialist. A close co-worker and friend of several years recalls that he was talking about land reform in the Mississippi Delta as far back as 1963, when most of his associates thought "the nigger must be crazy talking about us taking over Eastland's plantation." In the 1966 article, "Power and Racism," from which the opening quote was taken, he discusses the need to destroy capitalism, develop undying love within the black community and to develop a communal system among blacks.

At Berkeley he discussed the impossibility of economically insecure blacks building coalitions with the economically secure "liberal" whites. He spoke of our hooking up with black people around the world—not only psychologically but in terms of concrete working relationships.

In 1967 at the Latin American Solidarity Conference, he emphasized the fact that our language and cultural links with Africa had been broken in the same way that white Europeans force their language and culture on Latins living in the United States.

At the "Free Huey" rally in Oakland, California, in February 1968, Carmichael began to sharpen the concept that all persons of African descent, regardless of where they were born or lived, are Africans, that we must develop the concept of "undying love" for our people, and the necessity of joining the nine hundred million Africans scattered around the globe. Further, he began stressing the need for acquiring "a piece of land."

Before the national Arab Student Conference in the autumn of 1968, he spoke about our fighting to defend Egypt, which is a part of Africa.

In Greensboro, North Carolina, right before leaving for Africa, he stressed the need for us to move past the "entertainment stage" of shouting about "how bad we are" and begin to engage in hard, serious analytical study if we were serious about revolution.

Thus, throughout these speeches, from 1965 to 1971, there are common threads, some of which are later discarded and others developed and strengthened. This does not imply that the reader will not find contradictions. There are bound to be contradictions in anyone's ideas and philosophy as each new day, week, month and year teaches us something new and clarifies a past misconception. To all who approach this book with an open mind, anxious to learn what the enigmatic Stokely Carmichael is all about, "where he's coming from," and how he arrived at his present mission and ideology, I think this volume offers some clear answers and insights. Even his enemies and those ready to believe the worst about any fellow black man may be in for a surprise and learn something if they are willing to put their own ideas to a test and meet the challenge. And to be honest, most of us do find Carmichael's ideas and plans to be a challenge, which too many of us are afraid to face.

It has indeed been difficult to choose the speeches and articles included here. In Montreal, Canada, in 1968, at the Black Writers Conference, near pandemonium broke out as he spoke, yet we were unable to include this particular speech. Likewise we have not included the many speeches given in Guyana or Africa, where he has always been received as a head of state and given a joyous welcome by Africans from all walks of life. The reader should note that large sections were edited out of several speeches to avoid repetitions where the same ideas are discussed adequately in other speeches. For instance, large segments were taken out of the OLAS speech because they duplicated what he had just finished saying at the Dialectics of Liberation Conference in London, which is recorded in the previous chapter. So, too, have large segments been extracted from the Greensboro, North Carolina, speech.

The difference in delivery style before black audiences and before white audiences is striking—thus one will be aware of the warmth and rapport which existed when he spoke before black groups. At the same time, the printed speeches cannot help losing much of their fire and enthusiasm of delivery since it is impossible to transmit audience reaction and all of Stokely's quips onto paper.

In the "Free Huey" speech, the author chose to edit out the lines claiming that "socialism and communism are irrelevant to the struggle of black people." When he said this, Stokely was referring to the sterile, stale brand of European Marxism-Leninism which so many "white radicals" in this country were and still are trying to push among black activists—an ideology which does not deal with the twentieth-century realities of racism and world racial polarization. Further, it completely ignores the fact that socialism has its roots in African communal systems. Because his statement made at the rally was not clarified at the time, he felt it better to delete it from the speech—as was done on his recently released record titles "Free Huey."

I would like to add that the publishers, following the normal editorial procedure, have excluded all the speech openings where Stokely usually introduced co-workers and associates traveling with him at the time. In many cases I am sure that Stokely would want their names mentioned here because of their valuable services to him and the contributions to the struggle which they have made and continued to make. Such persons would included Carver "Chico" Neblett, Cleveland "Cleve" Sellers, Jan Bailey, William "Winky" Hall, and Jean "Koko" Hughes Farrow. I hope that any I have overlooked will forgive me. I must add that in Montreal, Atlanta, and wherever his wife is present, Miriam has always been introduced by the host group as "first lady of the Black World" and so acknowledged by the audience.

The editor wishes to thank the following brothers and sisters for their assistance when urgently needed: Florence Tate, for her advice and assistance with the editing; Freddie Greene Biddle, for supplying detailed data on SNCC's early activities and Carmichael's early years in the movement; Jan Bailey, for making his Carmichael speech collection available to me; and to David Brothers, who has come through always on short notice and helped me deliver copy to meet last-minute deadlines.

We all hope that careful reading of this book will spur our brothers and sisters on to begin the challenging task of serious study, analysis and planning that lie ahead of us. We know it will be read and discussed, because to do otherwise would only perpetuate the ignorance and confusion which presently surrounds Stokely Carmichael the man and his ideas. That he has made mistakes and has his faults only confirms that he is indeed human.

Few other black men in our generation have inspired the love, respect, fear, and hatred which Stokely inspires among our people. And I do not exaggerate. The love and/or respect is clearly shown when three thousand blacks jam Howard University's auditorium, which seats fifteen hundred, to hear him speak. It is shown when our people plead with him to come back to the United States, saying how badly he is needed here. The fear, which frequently inspires hatred, is clearly evident by the amount of time, energy and money which his enemies spend attempting to discredit him. It is up to you, the reader, to find out what it's all about.

—Ethel N. Minor

Acknowledgments

I wish to thank Miss Elizabeth Sutherland Martinez for her invaluable help with the essays "Who Is Qualified?" and "Power and Racism."

A very special thank-you to my brother and colleague Michael ("Mike") Thelwell for his help with *Towards Black Liberation.*

I would like to thank my mother, May Charles, who served as my messenger.

I wish to express my gratitude to Sister Florence Tate for her assistance in reading and editing the manuscript.

And, of course, Ethel Minor, who not only served as editor and personal secretary, but also as political adviser—a true sister dedicated to our revolutionary struggle.

Naturally I must thank my wife, Zenzi, who has served and continues to serve as my everything.

Contents

Contents

STOKELY SPEAKS

1

Notes
About
a Class

BY JANE STEMBRIDGE

The most important class was "Stokely's speech class."
He put eight sentences on the blackboard, with a line between, like this:

I digs wine	I enjoy drinking cocktails
The peoples wants freedom	The people want freedom

Waveland, Mississippi, Work-Study Institute, February–March,
1965.
Reprinted from *The New Radicals: A Report with Documents*, by
Paul Jacobs and Saul Landau (New York: Vintage, 1966).

Whereinsoever the policemens goes they causes troubles	Anywhere the officers of the law go, they cause trouble
I wants to reddish to vote	I want to register to vote

STOKELY What do you think about these sentences? Such as—The peoples wants freedom?

ZELMA It doesn't sound right.

STOKELY What do you mean?

ZELMA "Peoples" isn't right.

STOKELY Does it mean anything?

MILTON People means everybody. Peoples means everybody in the world.

ALMA Both sentences are right as long as you understand them.

HENRY They're both okay, but in a speech class you have to use correct English.
(*Stokely writes "correct English" in corner of blackboard.*)

ZELMA I was taught at least to use the sentences on the right side.

STOKELY Does anybody you know use the sentences on the left?

CLASS Yes.

STOKELY Are they wrong?

ZELMA In terms of English, they are wrong.

STOKELY Who decides what is correct English and what is incorrect English?

MILTON People made rules. People in England, I guess.

4

STOKELY You all say some people speak like on the left side of the board. Could they go anywhere and speak that way? Could they go to Harvard?

CLASS Yes . . . No.

STOKELY Does Mr. Turnbow speak like on the left side?

CLASS Yes.

STOKELY Could Mr. Turnbow go to Harvard and speak like that? "I wants to reddish to vote."

CLASS Yes.

STOKELY Would he be embarrassed?

CLASS Yes . . . No!

ZELMA He wouldn't be, but I would. It doesn't sound right.

STOKELY Suppose someone from Harvard came to Holmes County and said, "I want to register to vote?" Would they be embarrassed?

ZELMA No.

STOKELY Is it embarrassing at Harvard but not in Holmes County? The way you speak?

MILTON It's inherited. It's depending on where you come from. The people at Harvard would understand.

STOKELY Do you think the people at Harvard should forgive you?

MILTON The people at Harvard should help teach us correct English.

ALMA Why should we change if we understand what we mean?

SHIRLEY It is embarrassing.

5

STOKELY   Which way do most people talk?

CLASS   Like on the left.
(*He asks each student. All but two say "Left." One says that Southerners speak like on the left, Northerners on the right. Another says that Southerners speak like on the left, but the majority of people speak like on the right.*)

STOKELY   Which way do television and radio people speak?

CLASS   Left.
(*There was a distinction made by the class between Northern commentators and local programs. Most programs were local and spoke like on the left, they said.*)

STOKELY   Which way do teachers speak?

CLASS   On the left, except in class.

STOKELY   If most people speak on the left, why are they trying to change these people?

GLADYS   If you don't talk right, society rejects you. It embarrasses other people if you don't talk right.

HANK   But Mississippi society, ours, isn't embarrassed by it.

SHIRLEY   But the middle class wouldn't class us with them.

HANK   They won't accept "reddish." What is reddish? It's Negro dialect and it's something you eat.

STOKELY   Will society reject you if you don't speak like on the right side of the board? Gladys said society would reject you.

GLADYS   You might as well face it, man! What we gotta do is go out and become middle class. If you can't speak good English, you don't have a car, a job, or anything.

STOKELY If society rejects you because you don't speak good English, should you learn to speak good English?

CLASS No!

ALMA I'm tired of doing what society say. Let society say "reddish" for a while. People ought to just accept each other.

ZELMA I think we should be speaking just like we always have.

ALMA If I change for society, I wouldn't be free anyway.

ERNESTINE I'd like to learn correct English for my own sake.

SHIRLEY I would too.

ALMA If the majority speaks on the left, then a minority must rule society. Why do we have to change to be accepted by the minority group?
(*Lunchtime.*)

STOKELY Let's think about two questions for next time: What is society? Who makes the rules for society?

The class lasted a little more than an hour. It moved very quickly. It was very good. That is, people learned. I think they learned because:
—people learn from someone they trust, who trusts them. This trust included Stokely's self-trust and trust, or seriousness, about the subject matter;
—people learn more, and more quickly, from induction rather than deduction;
—people learn when they themselves can make the connection between ideas; can move from here to here to here to there;
—people learn when learning situations emphasize and

7

develop one single idea, which is very important to them personally;
—people learn when they can see what they are talking about. Stokely used the board.

Among other things, they themselves concluded:
—there is something called "correct English" and something called "incorrect English";
—most people in the country use some form of incorrect or broken English;
—it is not embarrassing to these people themselves;
—it is made embarrassing by other people because it is embarrassing to them;
—they are a minority, the people who use correct English;
—they decide what is correct English;
—they make that important and use it to shame people and keep them out of society;
—they make that a requirement for jobs and acceptance;
—they decide who is acceptable to society, by shame; but not everybody can be shamed—not Mr. Turnbow, for example;
—the main thing is to understand what people mean when they talk;
—that is not the main thing to society;

I recorded the whole class because it is a whole thing— one thing. That is why people learned. At least, that is why I learned.

I don't want to make conclusions or proposals. I think Stokely's class can stand on its own. Not only that, I think it is better than anything I could say. Just two things: he spoke to where they were at, and they were at different places, and the places changed during the movement of the discussion. Secondly, he trusted them and he trusted himself . . . and they trusted him.

2

Who Is Qualified ?

"[Poverty] is no longer associated with immigrant groups with high aspirations; it is identified with those whose social existence makes it more and more difficult to break out into the larger society. At the same time, the educational requirements of the economy are increasing."
—MICHAEL HARRINGTON, *The Other America*

Lowndes County, Alabama

I wouldn't be the first to point out the American capacity for self-delusion. One of the main reasons for the criticism of American society by the Students for a Democratic Society, the Student Nonviolent Coordinating Committee and other groups is that our society is *exclusive* while maintaining that it is *inclusive*. Although automation has prompted some rethinking about the Alger myth and upward mobility, few people are realistic

New Republic, January 8, 1966.

about the ways in which one legally can "make it" here
—or who can make it.

The real ways are three: by having money, by knowing
the right people, and by education. The first two methods
cannot be acknowledged by most of our citizens or our
government because they are not available to everyone
and we want to think that everyone has equal opportunity
in the United States. Therefore, Americans compensate
for this by saying that at least there is education, and
that is available to anyone who cares enough.

The panacea for lack of opportunity is education, as is
the panacea for prejudice. But just how available is it? If
every sixteen-year-old in the nation were motivated to
attend high school, he could not: there are not enough
schools, not enough physical space. As for college, less
than one-quarter of the population ever gets there. The
financial barrier is too high; even the cheapest state
college charges fees which are impossible for the poor.
Scholarships serve only the gifted. To make matters
worse, many universities and colleges are already fighting
off the mob by making entry more difficult. It is getting
harder, not easier, for the poor to be included here. For
the Negro, there is an additional problem. He is not
psychologically attuned to think of college as a goal.
Society has taught him to set short sights for himself, and
so he does.

Hard work was once considered a fourth way to climb
the ladder, and some Americans still see it as a possibility. Automation should have buried that once and for
all: you can't start as an elevator operator and move up to
be the president of the company, because there are—or
soon will be—buttons instead of operators. Actually, the
hard-work method was finished off before automation—
but until today only a handful of social critics had the
nerve to say that ours was a nation of classes. You have to
start ahead of the pack to make that climb.

Think now of the Southern Negro, driven off the land in

increasing numbers today, coming to the Northern city. He can hardly be compared to previous immigrants, most of whom brought skills with them. Others took menial work until they could save up and open "a little shop." The Southern Negro arrives; is he to pick cotton in Manhattan? He finds the menial work automated and the "little shop" gobbled up by supermarkets. He is, in fact, unemployable—from the Mississippi Delta to Watts. As for finding work in the new factories of the "changing South," he can forget it; if anything, those factories will be more automated than others. As for education, he probably cannot even read or write because Southern Negro elementary schools are that bad. You have to pass tests to get into college; he doesn't even have the education to get an education. Civil rights protest has not materially benefited the masses of Negroes; it has helped those who were already just a little ahead. The main result of that protest has been an opening up of the society to Negroes who had one of the criteria for upward mobility. Jobs have opened up, but they are mainly the jobs on Madison Avenue or Wall Street—which require education. Housing has opened up, but mainly in the "better neighborhoods." In a sense, the Negroes helped by protest have been those who never wanted to be Negroes. Americans who would point to the occasional Negro in his $30,000 suburban home or his sports car and say, "He made it," should have met the Mississippi lady of color who said to me in 1962: "The food that Ralph Bunche eats doesn't fill my stomach."

The South is not some odd, unique corner of this nation; it is super-America. The Negro is not some "minority group," but a microcosm of the excluded. A white boy may sit with me watching the President on television, and think: I could be President. No such thought would have occurred to this black boy or any other. In fact the white boy is wrong: he doesn't have much chance either of becoming President. Unless he has money, the right

11

contacts or education, he too will be excluded. Racism is real enough in the United States, but exclusion is not based on race alone. There may be proportionately less Negroes than whites among the included; and Negroes are, of course, "last to be hired, first to be fired." But the number of excluded whites is vast. The three criteria for upward mobility apply brutally to black and white everywhere.

Let me make one thing clear: I am not saying that the goal is for Negroes and other excluded persons to be allowed to join the middle-class mainstream of American society as we see it today. Aside from the fact that at least some Negroes don't want that, such inclusion is impossible under present circumstances. For a real end to exclusion in American society, that society would have to be so radically changed that the goal cannot really be defined as inclusion. "They talk about participating in the mainstream," said a Brooklyn College faculty member recently at a teach-in on the anti-poverty program, "when they don't realize that the mainstream is the very cause of their troubles."

Education is one major form (and means) of exclusion; politics is another. Who plays politics in this country? People who have one of the three qualifications for inclusion. They tell us: "Register to vote and take over the political machines." But this is farcical; the only people who take over the machines are other political mechanics.

If there is doubt about the existence of exclusion from politics, the passage of the 1965 Voting Act should have established it. That legislation passed only because most Americans had finally recognized that such exclusion did exist. Readers familiar with the congressional challenge of the Mississippi Freedom Democratic Party will remember the exclusion—political and even physical—experienced by that group of Southern Negroes. But most Americans do not see that the Voting Act hasn't solved the problem. Recent reports of the Civil Rights Commission and other groups point up the need for more federal examiners and the need to inform Negroes of their rights if the Act is to be meaningful. Yet the attitude of the Justice Department suggests that the government is not yet willing to take the initiative necessary for registering Negroes who are not already free from fear and aware of their rights. The three criteria mentioned here—money, who you know, and especially education—are what people mean when they use the word *qualified*. After the Watts uprising, committees were assigned to study the causes and make recommendations. These were composed of the "experts on Negroes," the "qualified." I am not opposed to the presence on such committees of intellectuals and professionals or merely making a parallel objection to poverty boards that don't include the poor. My objection is to the basic approach, which excludes the unqualified.

Again, the Southern Negro is not unique but a microcosm. He has been shamed into distrusting his own capacity to grow and lead and articulate. He has been shamed from birth by his skin, his poverty, his ignorance and even his speech. Whom does he see on television? Who gets projected in politics? The Lindsays and the Rockefellers and even the Martin Luther Kings—but not the Fannie Lou Hamers.* That is why it was so important to project her during the MFDP challenge. Sharecroppers can identify with her. She opens up the hope that they too can be projected, because she says all the things that they

---

* Fannie Lou Hamer, a forty-five-year-old sharecropper who worked on a Sunflower County, Miss., plantation, was forced to leave after registering to vote. She was shot at several times, once in her own home, by whites in the area. As a Mississippi Freedom Democratic Party delegate to the 1964 National Democratic Party Convention in Atlantic City, N.J., Mrs. Hamer and other delegates tried to unseat "regular Democrats"—and failed. In 1965, she was badly beaten in the Winona, Miss., bus station—just after the civil rights bill had been passed.

Mrs. Hamer is presently engaged in a political race against Jamie Whitney (who has been in office for over twenty years) for Mississippi's second congressional seat in the U.S. Congress.

have been saying to themselves—but she is heard. Mrs. Hamer's significance is very different from Dr. King's. One hears white people say of Dr. King: "He is so intelligent, so articulate." Of Mrs. Hamer they say: "What a beautiful soul"—implying that she lacks analytical intelligence. To some extent, and sadly, Mrs. Hamer has come to accept this vision of herself. Those who know her, and others like her, feel that her intelligence is just as great and her analysis as sharp. But Dr. King has one of the three qualifications—education. This is no criticism of the man, but of the society.

When SNCC first went to work in Lowndes County, Alabama, I—a "qualified" person by virtue of my college education—used to say to the black people there that they should register to vote and then make their voices heard. They could assert their rights, take over the power structure. This was the prescription of the qualified. But these people said they didn't want to do that; they did not think they could; they did not even want to enter a machine headed by George Wallace. To them politics meant Wallace, Sheriff Jim Clark, and Tom Coleman, who had been accused of the murder of Jonathan Daniels. To them the Democratic Party didn't mean L.B.J., but a crew of racist bullies and killers. Entering politics meant, until last summer, confronting the tools of Wallace: the county registrars who had flunked Negroes consistently for years.

They asked if something different could not be created. They wanted to redefine politics, make up new rules, and play the game with some personal integrity. Out of a negative force, fear, grew the positive drive to think new. SNCC's research department provided the tool: an unusual Alabama law.

Local "freedom parties" are now being organized in ten counties stretching across Alabama's Black Belt, with plans to do this in twelve more counties. Together, they contain 40 per cent of the potential state vote. Given the

Flowers-Wallace contest,* which must come, the balance of power could lie with those counties. But the true excitement of this development lies in what it means for the people themselves. The meetings of the executive committees of these county parties are open. The parties will hold county conventions and draw up platforms in April 1966. Later, candidates will be nominated who must support those platforms. In conventional politics it is the candidates who spell out the platform (*i.e.*, make promises); in Alabama candidates won't have to out-promise each other, but simply represent.

Right now, workshops are being held to prepare for the future: 150 black Alabamans have already learned about the duties of a county sheriff and a tax assessor, with more to come. Very few citizens anywhere in this country know what such duties are.

Some say it is romantic to place faith in "the masses" as a force for radical change. But the people who say this are the "qualified." Alabama Negroes are beginning to believe they don't need to be qualified to get involved in politics. People long accustomed to self-contempt are beginning to believe in their own voice.

Others might say we are leading the black people of Alabama down the road to frustration. Perhaps power politics will eventually overwhelm the freedom parties and the would-be Negro sheriffs. But there are reasons why this might not happen in Alabama. In counties with Negro majorities, there could be a black sheriff elected next year. Even a Governor Wallace will have to deal with him. SNCC learned from the Mississippi Freedom Democratic Party experience that the Southern Negro doesn't have to cast his lot with the national Democratic Party in order to be recognized as a force which must be

---

* Flowers was the so-called "liberal" candidate running against Wallace for the governorship of Alabama.

dealt with. The Johnson administration pushed through the Voting Act on the assumption that Negroes would automatically line up with its party, but their allegiance is not quite guaranteed. In New York they cast crucial votes for Lindsay, and in the South both Democrats and Republicans are now vying for the Negro vote.

I have hope for this nation, but it is not based on the idea of an American consensus favorable to progress; James Baldwin's idea of the Negro as the conscience of the country is closer to the truth. The majority view is a lie, based on a premise of an upward mobility that doesn't exist for most Americans. They may think the government is at least dealing with basic problems (racial injustice, poverty), but it cannot solve them when it starts from the wrong premise.

The status quo persists because there are no ways up from the bottom. When improvements within the system have been made, they resulted from pressure—pressure from below. Nothing has been given away; governments don't hand out justice because it's a nice thing to do. People must struggle and die first: Goodman, Schwerner, and Chaney, and, in the county where I am working, Mrs. Viola Liuzzo and Jonathan Daniels.

President Johnson's concept of the Great Society is preposterous. The definition comes from him, as does the means of entering that society. Excluded people must acquire the opportunity to redefine what the Great Society is, and then it may have meaning. I place my own hope for the United States in the growth of belief among the unqualified that they are in fact qualified: they can articulate and be responsible and hold power.

3

Power
and
Racism

One of the tragedies of the struggle against racism is that up to now there has been no national organization that could speak to the growing militancy of young black people in the urban ghetto. There has been only a civil rights movement, whose tone of voice was adapted to an audience of liberal whites. It served as a sort of buffer zone between them and angry young blacks. None of its so-called leaders could go into a rioting community and be listened to. In a sense, I blame ourselves—together with the mass media—for what has happened in Watts, Harlem, Chicago, Cleveland, and Omaha. Each time the people in those cities saw Martin Luther King get slapped, they became angry; when they saw four little black girls bombed to death, they were angrier; and when nothing happened, they were steaming. We had nothing to offer that they could see, except to go out and be beaten again. We helped to build their frustration.

For too many years, black Americans marched and had their heads broken and got shot. They were saying to the country, "Look, you guys are supposed to be nice guys and we are only going to do what we are supposed to do—why do you beat us up, why don't you give us what we ask, why don't you straighten yourself out?" After years of this, we are at almost the same point—because we demonstrated from a position of weakness. We cannot be expected any longer to march and have our heads broken in order to say to whites: Come on, you're nice guys. For you are not nice guys. We have found you out.

An organization which claims to speak for the needs of a community—as does the Student Nonviolent Coordinating Committee—must speak in the tone of that community, not as somebody else's buffer zone. This is the significance of Black Power as a slogan. For once, black people are going to use the words they want to use—not just the words whites want to hear. And they will do this no matter how often the press tries to stop the use of the slogan by equating it with racism or separatism.

An organization which claims to be working for the needs of a community—as SNCC does—must work to provide that community with a position of strength from which to make its voice heard. This is the significance of Black Power beyond the slogan.

Black Power can be clearly defined for those who do not attach the fears of white America to their questions about it. We should begin with the basic fact that black Americans have two problems: they are poor and they are black. All other problems arise from this two-sided reality: lack of education, the so-called apathy of black men. Any program to end racism must address itself to that double reality.

Almost from its beginning, SNCC sought to address itself to both conditions with a program aimed at winning political power for impoverished Southern blacks. We had to begin with politics because black Americans are a propertyless people in a country where property is valued above all. We had to work for power, because this country does not function by morality, love, and nonviolence, but by power. Thus we determined to win political power, with the idea of moving on from there into activity that would have economic effects. With power, the masses could *make or participate in making* the decisions which govern their destinies, and thus create basic change in their day-to-day lives.

But if political power seemed to be the key to self-determination, it was also obvious that the key had been thrown down a deep well many years earlier. Disenfranchisement, maintained by racist terror, made it impossible to talk about organizing for political power in 1960. The right to vote had to be won, and SNCC workers devoted their energies to this from 1961 to 1965. They set up voter registration drives in the Deep South. They created pressure for the vote by holding mock elections in Mississippi in 1963 and by helping to establish the Mississippi Freedom Democratic Party (MFDP) in 1964. That struggle was eased, though not won, with the passage of the 1965 Voting Rights Act. SNCC workers could then address themselves to the question: Who can we vote for, to have our needs met—how do we make our vote meaningful?

SNCC had already gone to Atlantic City for recognition of the Mississippi Freedom Democratic Party by the Democratic convention and been rejected; it had gone with the MFDP to Washington for recognition by Congress and been rejected. In Arkansas, SNCC helped thirty Negroes to run for school board elections; all but one were defeated, and there was evidence of fraud and intimidation sufficient to cause their defeat. In Atlanta, Julian Bond ran for the state legislature and was elected—twice—and unseated—twice. In several states, black farmers ran in elections for agricultural committees which make crucial decisions concerning land use, loans, etc. Although they won places on a number of committees, they never gained the majorities needed to control them.

All of the efforts were attempts to win Black Power. Then, in Alabama, the opportunity came to see how blacks could be organized on an independent party basis. An unusual Alabama law provides that any group of citizens can nominate candidates for county office, and if they win 20 per cent of the vote, may be recognized as a county political party. The same then applies on a state level. SNCC went to organize in several counties, such as Lowndes, where black people—who form 80 per cent of the population and have an average annual income of $943— felt they could accomplish nothing within the framework of the Alabama Democratic Party because of its racism and because the qualifying fee for the 1966 elections was raised from $50 to $500 in order to prevent most Negroes from becoming candidates. On May 3, 1966, five new county "freedom organizations" convened and nominated candidates for the offices of sheriff, tax assessor, members of the school boards.* Their ballot symbol was the black panther: a bold, beautiful animal, representing the strength and dignity of black demands today. A man needs a black panther on his side when he and his family must endure—as hundreds of Alabamans have endured—

* The Lowndes County Freedom Organization slate lost that election by a narrow margin amid much violence on election day. They received enough votes, however, to qualify as an official party in Alabama, and are now called the Lowndes County Freedom Party.

loss of job, eviction, starvation, and sometimes death for political activity. He may also need a gun, and SNCC reaffirms the right of black men everywhere to defend themselves when threatened or attacked. As for initiating the use of violence, we hope that such programs as ours will make that unnecessary; but it is not for us to tell black communities whether they can or cannot use any particular form of action to resolve their problems. Responsibility for the use of violence by black men, whether in self-defense or initiated by them, lies with the white community.

This is the specific historical experience from which SNCC's call for Black Power emerged on the Mississippi march in July 1966. But the concept of Black Power is not a recent or isolated phenomenon: it has grown out of the ferment of agitation and activity by different people and organizations in many black communities over the years. Our last year of work in Alabama added a new concrete possibility. In Lowndes County, for example, Black Power will mean that if a Negro is elected sheriff, he can end police brutality. If a black man is elected tax assessor, he can collect and channel funds for the building of better roads and schools serving black people—thus advancing the move from political power into the economic arena. In such areas as Lowndes, where black men have a majority, they will attempt to use it to exercise control. This is what they seek: control. Where Negroes lack a majority, Black Power means proper representation and sharing of control. It means the creation of power bases from which black people can work to change statewide or nationwide patterns of oppression through pressure from strength—instead of weakness. Politically, Black Power means what it has always meant to SNCC: the coming-together of black people to elect representatives and *to force those representatives to speak to their needs*. It does not mean merely putting black faces into office. A man or woman who is black and from the slums cannot be automatically expected to speak to the needs of black people. Most of the black politicians we see around the country today are not what SNCC means by Black Power. The power must be that of a community, and emanate from there.

SNCC today is working in both North and South on programs of voter registration and independent political organizing. In some places, such as Alabama, Los Angeles, New York, Philadelphia, and New Jersey, independent organizing under the black panther symbol is in progress. The creation of a national "black panther party" must come about; it will take time to build, and it is much too early to predict its success. We have no infallible master plan and we make no claim to exclusive knowledge of how to end racism; different groups will work in their own different ways. SNCC cannot spell out the full logistics of self-determination, but it can address itself to the problem by helping black communities define their needs, realize their strength, and go into action along a variety of lines which they must choose for themselves. Without knowing all the answers, it can address itself to the basic problem of poverty, to the fact that in Lowndes County 86 white families own 90 per cent of the land. What are black people in that county going to do for jobs; where are they going to get money? There must be reallocation of land, of money.

Ultimately, the economic foundations of this country must be shaken if black people are to control their lives. The colonies of the United States—and this includes the black ghettos within its borders, North and South—must be liberated. For a century, this nation has been like an octopus of exploitation, its tentacles stretching from Mississippi and Harlem to South America, the Middle East, southern Africa, and Vietnam; the form of exploitation varies from area to area but the essential result has been the same—a powerful few have been maintained and enriched at the expense of the poor and voiceless colored masses. This pattern must be broken. As its grip loosens here and there around the world, the hopes of black Americans become more realistic. For racism to die, a totally different America must be born.

This is what the white society does not wish to face; this is why that society prefers to talk about integration. But integration speaks not at all to the problem of poverty—only to the problem of blackness. Integration today means the man who "makes it," leaving his black brothers behind in the ghetto. It has no relevance to the Harlem wino or to the cottonpicker making three dollars a day.

Integration, moreover, speaks to the problem of blackness in a despicable way. As a goal, it has been based on complete acceptance of the fact that in order to have a decent house or education, blacks must move into a white neighborhood or send their children to a white school. This reinforces, among both black and white, the idea that "white" is automatically better and "black" is by definition inferior. This is why integration is a subterfuge for the maintenance of white supremacy. It allows the nation to focus on a handful of Southern children who get into white schools, at great price, and to ignore the 94 per cent who are left behind in unimproved all-black schools. Such situations will not change until black people have power—to control their own school boards, in this case. Then Negroes become equal in a way that means something, and integration ceases to be a one-way street. Then integration doesn't mean draining skills and energies from the ghetto into white neighborhoods; then it can mean white people moving from Beverly Hills into Watts, white people joining the Lowndes County Freedom Organization. Then integration becomes relevant.

In April 1966, before the furor over Black Power,

Christopher Jencks wrote in a *New Republic* article on white Mississippi's manipulation of the anti-poverty program:

> The war on poverty has been predicated on the notion that there is such a thing as *a community* which can be defined geographically and mobilized for a collective effort to help the poor. This theory has no relationship to reality in the Deep South. In every Mississippi county there are *two* communities. Despite all the pious platitudes of the moderates on both sides, these two communities habitually see their interests in terms of conflict rather than cooperation. Only when the Negro community can muster enough political, economic and professional strength to compete on somewhat equal terms, will Negroes believe in the possibility of true cooperation and whites accept its necessity. En route to integration, the Negro community needs to develop greater independence—a chance to run its own affairs and not cave in whenever "the man" barks . . . Or so it seems to me, and to most of the knowledgeable people with whom I talked in Mississippi. To OEO, this judgment may sound like black nationalism . . .

Mr. Jencks, a white reporter, perceived the reason why America's anti-poverty program has been a sick farce in both North and South. In the South, it is clearly racism which prevents the poor from running their own programs; in the North, it more often seems to be politicking and bureaucracy. But the results are not so different: in the North, non-whites make up 42 per cent of all families in metropolitan "poverty areas" and only 6 per cent of families in areas classified as not poor. SNCC has been working with local residents in Arkansas, Alabama, and Mississippi to achieve control by the poor of the program and its funds; it has also been working with groups in the North, and the struggle is no less difficult. Behind it all is a federal government which cares far more about winning the war on the Vietnamese than the war on poverty; which has put the poverty program in the hands of self-serving politicians and bureaucrats rather than the poor themselves; which is unwilling to curb the misuse of white power but quick to condemn Black Power.

To most whites, Black Power seems to mean that the Mau Mau are coming to the suburbs at night. The Mau Mau are coming, and whites must stop them. Articles appear about plots to "get Whitey," creating an atmosphere in which "law and order must be maintained." Once again, responsibility is shifted from the oppressor to the oppressed. Other whites chide, "Don't forget—you're only 10 per cent of the population; if you get too smart, we'll wipe you out." If they are liberals, they complain, "What about me—don't you want my help any more?" These are people supposedly concerned about black Americans, but today they think first of themselves, of their feelings of rejection. Or they admonish, "You can't get anywhere without coalitions," when there is in fact no group at present with whom to form a coalition in which blacks will not be absorbed and betrayed. Or they accuse us of "polarizing the races" by our calls for black unity, when the true responsibility for polarization lies with whites who will not accept their responsibility as the majority power for making the democratic process work.

White America will not face the problem of color, the reality of it. The well-intended say: "We're all human, everybody is really decent, we must forget color." But color cannot be "forgotten" until its weight is recognized and dealt with. White America will not acknowledge that the ways in which this country sees itself are contradicted by being black—and always have been. Whereas most of the people who settled this country came here for freedom or for economic opportunity, blacks were brought here to be slaves. When the Lowndes County Freedom Organization chose the black panther as its symbol, it was christened by the press "the Black Panther Party"—but the Alabama Democratic Party, whose symbol is a rooster, has never been called the White Cock Party. No one ever talked about "white power" because power in this country *is* white. All this adds up to more than merely identifying a group phenomenon by some catchy name or adjective. The furor over that black panther reveals the problems that white America has with color and sex; the furor over Black Power reveals how deep racism runs and the great fear which is attached to it.

Whites will not see that I, for example, as a person oppressed because of my blackness, have common cause with other blacks who are oppressed because of blackness. This is not to say that there are no white people who see things as I do, but that it is black people I must speak to first. It must be the oppressed to whom SNCC addresses itself primarily, not to friends from the oppressing group.

From birth, black people are told a set of lies about themselves. We are told that we are lazy—yet I drive through the Delta area of Mississippi and watch black people picking cotton in the hot sun for fourteen hours. We are told, "If you work hard, you'll succeed"—but if that were true, black people would own this country. We are oppressed because we are black—not because we are ignorant, not because we are lazy, not because we're stupid (and got good rhythm), but because we're black.

I remember that when I was a boy I used to go to see Tarzan movies on Saturday. White Tarzan used to beat up the black natives. I would sit there yelling, "Kill the beasts, kill the savages, kill 'em!" I was saying: Kill *me*. It was as if a Jewish boy watched Nazis taking Jews off to concentration camps and cheered them on. Today, I want the chief to beat hell out of Tarzan and send him back to Europe. But it takes time to become free of the lies and their shaming effect on black minds. It takes time to reject the most important lie: that black people inherently can't do the same things white people can do, unless white people help them.

The need for psychological equality is the reason why SNCC today believes that blacks must organize in the black community. Only black people can convey the revolutionary idea that black people are able to do things themselves. Only they can help create in the community an aroused and continuing black consciousness that will provide the basis for political strength. In the past, white allies have furthered white supremacy without the whites involved realizing it—or wanting it, I think. Black people must do things for themselves; they must get poverty money they will control and spend themselves, they must conduct tutorial programs themselves so that black children can identify with black people. This is one reason Africa has such importance: the reality of black men ruling their own nations gives blacks elsewhere a sense of possibility, of power, which they do not now have.

This does not mean we don't welcome help, or friends. But we want the right to decide whether anyone is, in fact, our friend. In the past, black Americans have been almost the only people whom everybody and his momma could jump up and call their friends. We have been tokens, symbols, objects—as I was in high school to many young whites, who liked having "a Negro friend." We want to decide who is our friend, and we will not accept someone who comes to us and says: "If you do X, Y, and Z, then I'll help you." We will not be told whom we should choose as allies. We will not be isolated from any group or nation except by our own choice. We cannot have the oppressors telling the oppressed how to rid themselves of the oppressor.

I have said that most liberal whites react to Black Power with the question, "What about me?" rather than saying: "Tell me what you want me to do and I'll see if I can do it." There are answers to the right question. One of the most disturbing things about almost all white supporters of the movement has been that they are afraid to go into their own communities—which is where the racism exists—and work to get rid of it. They want to run from Berkeley to tell us what to do in Mississippi; let them look instead at Berkeley. They admonish blacks to be nonviolent; let them preach nonviolence in the white community. They come to teach me Negro history; let them go to the suburbs and open up freedom schools for whites. Let them work to stop America's racist foreign policy; let them press this government to cease supporting the economy of South Africa.

There is a vital job to be done among poor whites. We hope to see, eventually, a coalition between poor blacks and poor whites. That is the only coalition which seems acceptable to us, and we see such a coalition as the major internal instrument of change in American society. SNCC has tried several times to organize poor whites; we are trying again now, with an initial training program in Tennessee. It is purely academic today to talk about bringing poor blacks and whites together, but the job of creating a poor-white power bloc must be attempted. The main responsibility for it falls upon whites. Black and white can work together in the white community where possible; it is not possible, however, to go into a poor Southern town and talk about integration. Poor whites everywhere are becoming more hostile—not less—partly because they see the nation's attention focused on black poverty and nobody coming to them. Too many young middle-class Americans, like some sort of Pepsi generation, have wanted to come alive through the black community; they've wanted to be where the action is—and the action has been in the black community.

Black people do not want to "take over" this country. They don't want to "get Whitey"; they just want to get him off their backs, as the saying goes. It was, for example, the exploitation by Jewish landlords and merchants which first created black resentment toward Jews—not Judaism. The white man is irrelevant to blacks, except as an oppressive force. Blacks want to be in his place, yes, but not in order to terrorize and lynch and starve him. They want to be in his place because that is where a decent life can be had.

But our vision is not merely of a society in which all black men have enough to buy the good things of life. When we urge that black money go into black pockets, we mean the communal pocket. We want to see money go back into the community and used to benefit it. We want to see the cooperative concept applied in business and banking. We want to see black ghetto residents demand that an exploiting landlord or storekeeper sell them, at minimal cost, a building or a shop that they will own and improve cooperatively; they can back their demand with a rent strike, or a boycott, and a community so unified behind them that no one else will move into the building or buy at the store. The society we seek to build among black people, then, is not a capitalist one. It is a society in which the spirit of community and humanistic love prevail. The word "love" is suspect; black expectations of what it might produce have been betrayed too often. But those were expectations of a response from the white community, which failed us. The love we seek to encourage is within the black community, the only American community where men call each other "brother" when they meet. We can build a community of love only where we have the ability and power to do so: among blacks.

As for white America, perhaps it can stop crying out against "black supremacy," "black nationalism," "racism in reverse," and begin facing reality. The reality is that this nation is racist; that racism is not primarily a problem of "human relations" but of an exploitation maintained—either actively or through silence—by the society as a whole. Can whites, particularly liberal whites, condemn themselves? Can they stop blaming us, and blame their own system? Are they capable of the shame which might become a revolutionary emotion? We have found that they usually cannot condemn themselves, and so we have done it. But the rebuilding of this society, if at all possible, is basically the responsibility of whites—not blacks. We won't fight to save the present society, in Vietnam or anywhere else. We are just going to work, in the way *we* see fit, and on goals *we* define, not for civil rights but for all our human rights.

4

Toward Black Liberation

One of the most pointed illustrations of the need for Black Power, as a positive and redemptive force in a society degenerating into a form of totalitarianism, is to be made by examining the history of distortion that the concept has been given by the national media of publicity. In this "debate," as in everything else that affects our lives, Negroes are dependent on, and at the discretion of, forces and institutions within the white society that have little interest in representing us honestly. Our experience with the national

Reprinted from *The Massachusetts Review*, September, 1966. Copyright © 1966 by The Student Nonviolent Coordinating Committee.

press has been that when they have managed to escape a meretricious special interest in "Git Whitey" sensationalism and race-war mongering, individual reporters and commentators have been conditioned by the enveloping racism of the society to the point where they are incapable of objective observation and reporting of racial *incidents*, much less the analysis of *ideas*. But this limitation of vision and perceptions is an inevitable consequence of the dictatorship of definition, interpretation, and consciousness, along with the censorship of history that the society has inflicted upon the Negro—and itself.

Our concern for Black Power addresses itself directly to this problem: the necessity to reclaim our history and our identity from the cultural terrorism and depredation of self-justifying white guilt.

To do this we shall have to struggle for the right to create our own terms to define ourselves and our relationship to the society, and to have these terms recognized. This is the first necessity of a free people, and the first right that any oppressor must suspend. The white fathers of American racism knew this—instinctively it seems—as is indicated by the continuous record of the distortion and omission in their dealings with the red and black men. In the same way that Southern apologists for the "Jim Crow" society have so obscured, muddied and misrepresented the record of the Reconstruction period, until it is almost impossible to tell what really happened, their contemporary counterparts are busy with the recent history of the civil rights movement.

In 1964, for example, the National Democratic Party, led by L. B. Johnson and Hubert H. Humphrey, cynically undermined the efforts of Mississippi's black population to achieve some degree of political representation. Yet, whenever the events of that convention are recalled by the press, one sees only the version fabricated by the press agents of the Democratic Party. A year later the House representatives in an even more vulgar display of political racism made a mockery of the political rights of Mississippi's Negroes when it failed to unseat the Mississippi delegation to the House—which had been elected through a process that methodically and systematically excluded over 450,000 voting-age Negroes, almost one-half of the total electorate of the state. Whenever this event is mentioned in print, it is in terms that leave one with the rather curious impression that somehow the oppressed Negro people of Mississippi are at fault for confronting the Congress with a situation in which they had no alternative but to endorse Mississippi's racist political practices. I am speaking now of the Mississippi Freedom Democratic Party.

I mention these two examples because, having been directly involved in them, I can see very clearly the discrepancies between what happened and the versions that are finding their way into general acceptance as a kind of popular mythology. The victimization of the Negro takes place in two phases: first it occurs in fact and deed; then, and this is equally sinister, in the official recording of those facts.

The Black Power program and concept being articulated by SNCC, CORE, and a host of community organizations in the ghettos of the North and South, has not escaped that process. The white press has been busy articulating their own analyses, their own interpretations and criticisms. For example, while the press has given wide and sensational dissemination to attacks made by figures in the civil rights movement—foremost among them are Roy Wilkins of the NAACP and Whitney Young of the Urban League—and to the hysterical ranting about black racism made by that political chameleon, Vice-President Humphrey, it has generally failed to give accounts of the reasonable and productive dialogue that is taking place in the Negro community, and in certain important areas in the white religious and intellectual community. A national committee of influential Negro

churchmen affiliated with the National Council of
Churches, despite their obvious respectability and responsibility, had to resort to a paid advertisement to articulate
their position, while anyone shouting the hysterical yap-
pings of "black racism" got ample space. Thus the American people have got at best a superficial and misleading
account of the very terms and tenor of this debate. I wish
to quote briefly from the statement by the national committee of churchmen, which I suspect the majority of
Americans will not have seen. This statement appeared
in the *New York Times,* July 31, 1966:

> We, an informal group of Negro Churchmen in
> America, are deeply disturbed about the crisis
> brought upon our country by historic distortions
> of important human realities in the controversy
> about "black power." What we see shining through
> the variety of rhetoric is not anything new but the
> same old problem of power and race which has
> faced our beloved country since 1619.
>
> . . . The conscience of black men is corrupted
> because, having no power to implement the de-
> mands of conscience, the concern for justice in the
> absence of justice becomes a chaotic self-sur-
> render. Powerlessness breeds a race of beggars.
> We are faced now with a situation where power-
> less conscience meets conscience-less power,
> threatening the very foundations of our Nation.
>
> . . . We deplore the overt violence of riots, but
> we feel it is more important to focus on the real
> sources of these eruptions. These sources may be
> abetted inside the Ghetto, but their basic cause lies
> in the silent and covert violence which white mid-
> dle-class America inflicts upon the victims of the
> inner city.
>
> . . . In short, the failure of American leaders
> to use American power to create equal opportunity

34

in life as well as law, this is the real problem and
not the anguished cry for black power.

. . . Without the capacity to participate with
power, i.e., to have some organized political and
economic strength to really influence people with
whom one interacts—integration is not meaningful.

. . . America has asked its Negro citizens to
fight for opportunity as individuals, whereas at
certain points in our history what we have needed
most has been opportunity for the whole group,
not just for selected and approved Negroes.

. . . We must not apologize for the existence of
this form of group power, for we have been oppressed as a group and not as individuals. We will
not find our way out of that oppression until both
we and America accept the need for Negro Americans, as well as for Jews, Italians, Poles, and white
Anglo-Saxon Protestants, among others, to have
and to wield group power.

Traditionally, for each new ethnic group, the route to
social and political integration in America's pluralistic
society has been through the organization of their own
institutions with which to represent their communal
needs within the larger society. This is simply stating
what the advocates of Black Power are saying. The
strident outcry, *particularly* from the liberal community,
that has been evoked by this proposal can be understood
only by examining the historic relationship between Negro
and white power in this country.

Negroes are defined by two forces: their blackness and
their powerlessness. There have been, traditionally, two
communities in America: the white community, which
controlled and defined the forms that all institutions
within the society would take, and the Negro community,
which has been excluded from participation in the power

decisions that shaped the society, and has traditionally been dependent upon and subservient to the white community.

This has not been accidental. The history of every institution of this society indicates that a major concern in the ordering and structuring of the society has been the maintaining of the Negro community in its condition of dependence and oppression. This has not been on the level of individual acts of discrimination—individual whites against individual Negroes—but total acts by the white community against the Negro community. This fact cannot be too strongly emphasized—that racist assumptions of white superiority have been so deeply ingrained in the structure of the society that it infuses its entire functioning, and is so much a part of the national subconscious that it is taken for granted and is frequently not even recognized. It is more than a figure of speech to say that the Negro community in America is the victim of white imperialism and colonial exploitation.

It is white power that makes the laws, and it is violent white power in the form of armed white cops that enforces those laws with guns and nightsticks. The vast majority of Negroes in this country live in captive communities and must endure these conditions of oppression because, and only because, *they are black and powerless.* Without bothering to go into the historic factors that contribute to this pattern—economic exploitation, political impotence, discrimination in employment and education—one can see that to correct this pattern will require far-reaching changes in the basic power-relationships and the ingrained social patterns within the society. The question, of course, is: What kinds of changes are necessary, and how is it possible to bring them about?

In recent years the answer to these questions that has been given by most articulate groups of Negroes and their white allies, the "liberals" of all stripes, has been in terms of something called "integration." According to the advocates of integration, social justice will be accomplished by "integrating the Negro into the mainstream institutions of the society from which he has been traditionally excluded." It is very significant that each time I have heard this formulation it has been in terms of "the Negro," the individual Negro, rather than in terms of the community.

This concept of integration had to be based on the assumption that there was nothing of value in the Negro community, so the thing to do was to siphon off the "acceptable" Negroes into the surrounding middle-class white community. It is true that the student demonstrations in the South during the early sixties, out of which SNCC came, had a similar orientation. But while it is hardly a concern of a black sharecropper, dishwasher, or welfare recipient whether a certain fifteen-dollar-a-day motel offers accommodations to Negroes, the overt symbols of white superiority and the imposed limitations on the Negro community had to be destroyed. Now black people must look beyond these goals, to the issue of collective power.

Such a limited class orientation was reflected not only in the program and goals of the civil rights movement, but in its tactics and organization. It is very significant that the two oldest and most "respectable" civil rights organizations have constitutions which *specifically* prohibit partisan political activity. CORE once did, but changed that clause when it changed its orientation toward Black Power. But this is perfectly understandable in terms of the strategy and goals of the older organizations. The civil rights movement saw its role as a kind of liaison between the powerful white community and the dependent Negro one. The dependent status of the black community apparently was unimportant since—if the movement was successful—it was going to blend into the white community anyway. We made no pretense of organizing and developing institutions of community power in the Negro community, but appealed to the conscience of white institutions of power. The posture of the civil rights movement was that of the dependent, the suppliant. The theory was that without attempting to create any organized base of political strength itself, the civil rights movement could influence national legislation and national social patterns by forming coalitions with various "liberal" pressure organizations in the white community —liberal reform clubs, labor unions, church groups, progressive civic groups, and at times one or other of the major political parties.

I think we all have seen the limitations of this approach. We have repeatedly seen that political alliances based on appeals to conscience and decency are chancy things, simply because institutions and political organizations have no consciences outside their own special interests. The political and social rights of Negroes have been and always will be negotiable and expendable the moment they conflict with the interests of our "allies." If we do not learn from history, we are doomed to repeat it, and that is precisely the lesson of the Reconstruction. Black people were allowed to register, vote, and participate in politics because it was to the advantage of powerful white allies to promote this. But this was the result of white decision, and it was ended by other white men's decision before any political base powerful enough to challenge that decision could be established in the Southern Negro community. (Thus at this point in the struggle Negroes have no assurance—save a kind of idiot optimism and faith in a society whose history is one of racism—that if it were to become necessary, even the painfully limited gains thrown to the civil rights movement by the Congress will not be revoked as soon as a shift in political sentiments should occur.)

The major limitation of this approach was that it tended to maintain the traditional dependence of Negroes, and of the movement. We depended upon the good will and support of various groups within the white community whose interests were not always compatible with ours. To the extent that we depended on the financial support of other groups, we were vulnerable to their influence and domination.

Also, the program that evolved out of this coalition was really limited and inadequate in the long term, and one which affected only a small select group of Negroes. Its goal was to make the white community accessible to "qualified" Negroes and presumably each year a few more Negroes armed with their passport—a couple of university degrees—would escape into middle-class America and adopt the attitudes and life styles of that group; and one day the Harlems and the Watts would stand empty, a tribute to the success of integration. This is simply neither realistic nor particularly desirable. You can integrate communities, but you assimilate individuals. Even if such a program were possible its result would be, not to develop the black community as a functional and honorable segment of the total society, with its own cultural identity, life patterns, and institutions, but to abolish it— the final solution to the Negro problem. Marx said that the working class is the first class in history that ever wanted to abolish itself. If one listens to some of our "moderate" Negro leaders it appears that the American Negro is the first *race* that ever wished to abolish itself. The fact is that what must be abolished is not the black community, but the dependent colonial status that has been inflicted upon it. The racial and cultural personality of the black community must be preserved and the community must win its freedom while preserving its cultural integrity. This is the essential difference between integration as it is currently practiced and the concept of Black Power.

What has the movement for integration accomplished to date? The Negro graduating from M.I.T. with a doctorate will have better job opportunities available to him than to Lynda Bird Johnson. But the rate of unemployment in the Negro community is steadily increasing, while that in the white community decreases. More educated Negroes hold executive jobs in major corporations and federal agencies than ever before, but the gap between white income and Negro income has almost doubled in the last twenty years. More suburban housing is available to Negroes, but housing conditions in the ghetto are steadily declining. While the infant mortality rate of New York City is at its lowest rate ever in the city's history, the infant mortality rate of Harlem is steadily climbing. There has been an organized national resistance to the Supreme Court's order to integrate the schools, and the federal government has not acted to enforce that order. Less than 15 per cent of black children in the South attend integrated schools; and Negro schools, which the vast majority of black children still attend, are increasingly decrepit, overcrowded, understaffed, inadequately equipped and funded.

The rate of school dropouts is increasing among Negro teenagers, who then express their bitterness, hopelessness, and alienation by the only means they have—rebellion. As long as people in the ghettos of our large cities feel that they are victims of the misuse of white power without any way to have their needs represented—and these are frequently simple needs (to get the welfare inspectors to stop kicking down your doors in the middle of the night, the cops to stop beating your children, to get the landlord to exterminate the vermin in your home, the city to collect your garbage)—we will continue to have riots. These are not the products of Black Power, but of the absence of any organization capable of giving the community the power, the Black Power, to deal with its problems.

SNCC proposes that it is now time for the black freedom movement to stop pandering to the fears and anxieties of the white middle class in the attempt to earn its "good will," and to return to the ghetto to organize these communities to control themselves. This organization must be attempted in Northern and Southern urban areas as well as in the rural black-belt counties of the South. The chief antagonist to this organization is, in the South, the overtly racist Democratic Party, and in the North the equally corrupt big city machines.

The standard argument presented against independent political organization is, "But you are only 10 per cent." I cannot see the relevance of this observation, since no one is talking about taking over the country, but taking control over our own communities.

The fact is that the Negro population, 10 per cent or not, is very strategically placed because of—ironically—segregation. What is also true is that Negroes have never been able to utilize the full voting potential of our numbers. Where we can vote, the case has always been that the white political machine stacks and gerrymanders the political subdivisions in Negro neighborhoods, so the true voting strength is never reflected in political strength. Would anyone looking at the distribution of political power in Manhattan ever think that Negroes represented 60 per cent of the population there?

Just as often the effective political organization in Negro communities is absorbed by tokenism and patronage—the time-honored practice of "giving" certain offices to selected Negroes. The machine thus creates a "little machine," which is subordinate and responsive to it, in the Negro community. These Negro political "leaders" are really vote deliverers, more responsible to the white machine and the white power structure than to the community they allegedly represent. Thus the white community is able to substitute patronage control for audacious Black Power in the Negro community.

This is precisely what Johnson tried to do even before the Voting Rights Act of 1966 was passed. The national Democrats made it very clear that the measure was intended to register Democrats, not Negroes. The President and top officials of the Democratic Party called in almost one hundred selected Negro "leaders" from the Deep South. Nothing was said about changing the policies of the racist state parties, nothing was said about repudiating such leadership figures as Eastland and Ross Barnett in Mississippi or George Wallace in Alabama. What was said was simply, "Go home and organize your people into the local Democratic Party—*then* we'll see about poverty money and appointments." (Incidentally, for the most part the war on poverty in the South is controlled by local Democratic ward heelers—outspoken racists who have used the program to change the form of the Negroes' dependence. People who were afraid to register for fear of being thrown off the farm are now afraid to register for fear of losing their children's Head Start places.)

We must organize black community power to end these abuses, and to give the Negro community a chance to have its needs expressed. A leadership that is truly "responsible"—not to the white press and power structure, but to the community—must be developed. Such leadership will recognize that its power lies in the unified and collective strength of that community. This will make it difficult for the white leadership group to conduct its dialogue with individuals in terms of patronage and prestige, and will force them to talk to the community's representatives in terms of real power.

The single aspect of the Black Power program that has encountered most criticism is this concept of independent organization. This is presented as third-partyism which has never worked, or a withdrawal into black nationalism and isolationism. If such a program is developed it will not have the effect of isolating the Negro community but the reverse. When the Negro community is able to control local offices, and negotiate with other groups from a position of organized strength, the possibility of meaningful political alliances on specific issues will be increased. That is a rule of politics and there is no reason why it should not operate here. The only difference is that we will have the power to define the terms of these alliances.

The next question usually is, "So—can it work, can the ghettos in fact be organized?" The answer is that this organization must be successful, because there are no viable alternatives—not the war on poverty, which was at its inception limited to dealing with effects rather than causes, and has become simply another source of machine patronage. And "integration" is meaningful only to a small chosen class within the community.

The revolution in agricultural technology in the South is displacing the rural Negro community into Northern urban areas. Both Washington, D.C., and Newark have Negro majorities. One-third of Philadelphia's population of two million people is black. "Inner city" in most major urban areas is already predominantly Negro, and with the white rush to suburbia, Negroes will in the next three decades control the heart of our great cities. These areas can become either concentration camps with a bitter and volatile population, whose only power is the power to destroy, or organized and powerful communities able to make constructive contributions to the total society. Without the power to control their lives and their communities, without effective political institutions through which to relate to the total society, these communities will exist in a constant state of insurrection. This is a choice that the country will have to make.

5

Berkeley
Speech

It's a privilege and an honor to be in the white intellectual
ghetto of the West. This is a student conference, as it
should be, held on a campus, and we'll never be caught up
in intellectual masturbation on the question of Black
Power. That's a function of the people who are adver-
tisers but call themselves reporters. Incidentally, for my
friends and members of the press, my self-appointed
white critics, I was reading Mr. Bernard Shaw two days
ago, and I came across a very important quote that I

University of California, Berkeley, October, 1966.

think is most apropos to you. He says, "All criticism is an autobiography." Dig yourself. OK.

The philosophers Camus and Sartre raise the question of whether or not a man can condemn himself. The black existentialist philosopher who is pragmatic, Frantz Fanon, answered the question. He said that man could not. Camus and Sartre don't answer the question. We in SNCC tend to agree with Fanon—a man cannot condemn himself. If he did, he would then have to inflict punishment upon himself. An example is the Nazis. Any of the Nazi prisoners who, after he was caught and incarcerated, admitted that he committed crimes, that he killed all the many people he killed, had to commit suicide. The only ones able to stay alive were the ones who never admitted that they committed a crime against people— that is, the ones who rationalized that Jews were not human beings and deserved to be killed, or that they were only following orders. There's another, more recent example provided by the officials and the population—the white population—of Neshoba County, Mississippi (that's where Philadelphia is). They could not condemn Sheriff Rainey, his deputies, and the other fourteen men who killed three human beings. They could not because they elected Mr. Rainey to do precisely what he did; and condemning him would be condemning themselves.

In a much larger view, SNCC says that white America cannot condemn herself for her criminal acts against black America. So black people have done it—you stand condemned. The institutions that function in this country are clearly racist; they're built upon racism. The questions to be dealt with then are: How can black people inside this country move? How can white people who say they're not part of those institutions begin to move? And how then do we begin to clear away the obstacles that we have in this society, to make us live like human beings?

Several people have been upset because we've said that integration was irrelevant when initiated by blacks, and that in fact it was an insidious subterfuge for the maintenance of white supremacy. In the past six years or so, this country has been feeding us a "thalidomide drug of integration," and some Negroes have been walking down a dream street talking about sitting next to white people. That does not begin to solve the problem. We didn't go to Mississippi to sit next to Ross Barnett [former Governor of Mississippi], we did not go to sit next to Jim Clark [sheriff of Selma, Alabama], we went to get them out of our way. People ought to understand that; we were never fighting for the right to integrate, *we were fighting against white supremacy*. In order to understand white supremacy we must dismiss the fallacious notion that white people can give anybody his freedom. A man is born free. You may enslave a man after he is born free, and that is in fact what this country does. It enslaves blacks after they're born. The only thing white people can do *is stop denying black people their freedom*.

I maintain that every civil rights bill in this country was passed for white people, not for black people. For example, I am black. I know that. I also know that while I am black I am a human being. Therefore I have the right to go into any public place. White people didn't know that. Every time I tried to go into a public place they stopped me. So some boys had to write a bill to tell that white man, "He's a human being; don't stop him." That bill was for the white man, not for me. I knew I could vote all the time and that it wasn't a privilege but my right. Every time I tried I was shot, killed or jailed, beaten or economically deprived. So somebody had to write a bill to tell white people, "When a black man comes to vote, don't bother him." That bill was for white people. I know I can live anyplace I want to live. It is white people across this country who are incapable of allowing me to live where I want. You need a civil rights bill, not me. The failure of the civil rights bill isn't because of Black Power or because of the Student Nonviolent Coordinating Committee or because of the rebellions that are occurring in the major cities. That failure is due to the whites' incapacity to deal with their own problems inside their own communities. And so in a sense we must ask, How is it that black people move? And what do we do? But the question in a much greater sense is, How can white people who are the majority, and who are responsible for making democracy work, make it work? They have failed miserably on this point. They have never made democracy work, be it inside the United States, Vietnam, South Africa, the Philippines, South America, Puerto Rico, or wherever America has been. We not only condemn the country for what it has done internally, but we must condemn it for what it does externally. We see this country trying to rule the world, and someone must stand up and start articulating that this country is not God, and that it cannot rule the world.

The white supremacist attitude, which you have either consciously or subconsciously, is running rampant through society today. For example, missionaries were sent to Africa with the attitude that blacks were automatically inferior. As a matter of fact, the first act the missionaries did when they got to Africa was to make us cover up our bodies, because they said it got them excited. We couldn't go bare-breasted any more because they got excited! When the missionaries came to civilize us because we were uncivilized, to educate us because we were uneducated, and to give us some literate studies because we were illiterate, they charged a price. The missionaries came with the Bible, and we had the land; when they left, they had the land, and we still have the Bible. That's been the rationalization for Western civilization as it moves across the world—stealing, plundering and raping everybody in its path. Their one rationalization is that the rest of the world is uncivilized and they are in fact civilized. But the West is un-civ-i-lized. And that still runs on today, you see, because now we have "modern-day missionaries," and they come into our ghettos—they Head Start, Upward Lift, Bootstrap, and Upward Bound us into white society. They don't want to face the real problem. A man is poor for one reason and one reason only—he does not have money. If you want to get rid of poverty, you give people money. And you ought not to tell me about people who don't work, and that you can't give people money if they don't work, because if that were true, you'd have to start stopping Rockefeller, Kennedy, Lyndon Baines Johnson, Lady Bird Johnson, the whole of Standard Oil, the Gulf Corporation, all of them, including probably a large number of the board of trustees of this university. The question, then, is not whether or not one can work; it's *Who has power to make his or her acts legitimate?* That is all. In this country that power is invested in the hands of white people, and it makes their acts legitimate.

We are now engaged in a psychological struggle in this country about whether or not black people have the right to use the words they want to use without white people giving their sanction. We maintain the use of the words Black Power—let them address themselves to that. We are not going to wait for white people to sanction Black Power. We're tired of waiting; every time black people try to move in this country, they're forced to defend their position beforehand. It's time that white people do that. They ought to start defending themselves as to why they have oppressed and exploited us. A man was picked as a slave for one reason—the color of his skin. Black was automatically inferior, inhuman, and therefore fit for slavery, so the question of whether or not we are individually suppressed is nonsensical, and it's a downright lie. We are oppressed as a group because we are black, not because we are lazy or apathetic, not because we're stupid or we stink, not because we eat watermelon or have good rhythm. We are oppressed because we are black.

49

In order to escape that oppression we must wield the group power we have, not the individual power that this country sets as the criterion under which a man may come into it. That's what is called integration. "You do what I tell you to do and we'll let you sit at the table with us." Well, if you believe in integration, you can come live in Watts, send your children to the ghetto schools. Let's talk about that. If you believe in integration, then we're going to start adopting us some white people to live in our neighborhoods. So it is clear that this question is not one of integration or segregation. We cannot afford to be concerned about the 6 per cent of black children in this country whom you allow to enter white schools. We are going to be concerned about the 94 per cent. You ought to be concerned about them too. But are we willing to be concerned about the black people who will never get to Berkeley, never get to Harvard, and cannot get an education, the ones you'll never get a chance to rub shoulders with and say, "Why, he's almost as good as we are; he's not like the others"? The question is, How can white society begin to move to see black people as human beings? I am black, therefore I am. Not: I am black and I must go to college to prove myself. I am black, therefore I am. And don't deprive me of anything and say to me that you must go to college before you gain access to X, Y, and Z. That's only a rationalization for suppression.

The political parties of this country do not meet the needs of the people on a day-to-day basis. How can we build new political institutions that will become the political expressions of people? How can you build political institutions that will begin to meet the needs of Oakland, California? The need of Oakland, California, is not 1,000 policemen with submachine guns. They need that least of all. How can we build institutions that will allow those people to function on a day-to-day basis, so that they can get decent jobs and have decent houses, and they can begin to participate in the policy and make the decisions that affect their lives? That's what they need, not Gestapo troops, because this is not 1942, and if you play like Nazis, we're not going to play Jew this time around. Get hip to that. Can white people move inside their own community and start tearing down racism where in fact it exists? It is you who live in Cicero and stopped us from living there. White people stopped us from moving into Grenada, Miss. White people make sure that we live in the ghettos of this country. White institutions do that. They must change. In order for America to really live on a basic principle of human relationships, a new society must be born. Racism must die. The economic exploitation by this country of non-white people around the world must also die.

There are several programs in the South where whites are trying to organize poor whites so they can begin to move around the question of economic exploitation and political disfranchisement. We've all heard the theory several times. But few people are willing to go into it. The question is, Can the white activist stop trying to be a Pepsi generation who comes alive in the black community, and be a man who's willing to move into the white community and start organizing where the organization is needed? Can he do that? Can the white activist disassociate himself from the clowns who waste time parrying with each other and start talking about the problems that are facing people in this state? You must start inside the white community. Our political position is that we don't think the Democratic Party represents the needs of black people. We know that it does not. If, in fact, white people believe that they're going to move inside that structure, how are they going to organize around a concept of whiteness based on true brotherhood and on stopping economic exploitation in order to form a coalition base for black people to hook up with? You cannot build a coalition based on national sentiment. If you want a coalition to address itself to real changes in this country, white people must start building those institutions inside the white community. And that's the real question facing the white activists today. Can they tear down the institutions that have put us all in the trick bag we've been into for the last hundreds of years? Frederick Douglass said that the youth should fight to be leaders today. God knows we need to be leaders today, because the men who run this country are sick. We must begin to start building those institutions and to fight to articulate our position, to fight to be able to control our universities (we need to be able to do that), to fight to control the basic institutions that perpetuate racism by destroying them and building new ones. That's the real question that faces us today, and it is a dilemma because most of us don't know how to work.

Most white activists run into the black community as an excuse. We cannot have white people working in the black community—on psychological grounds. The fact is that all black people question whether or not they are equal to whites, since every time they start to do something, white people are around showing them how to do it. If we are going to eliminate that for the generation that comes after us, then black people must be in positions of power, doing and articulating for themselves. That's not reverse racism; it is moving onto healthy ground; it is becoming what the philosopher Sartre says, an "antiracist racist." And this country can't understand that. What we have in SNCC is antiracist racism. We are against racists. If everybody who's white sees himself as racist and sees us against him, he's speaking from his own guilt.

We do not have the power in our hands to change the institution of war in this country—to begin to re-create it so that they learn to leave the Vietnamese people alone. The only power we have is the power to say, "Hell, no!" to the draft.

The war in Vietnam is illegal and immoral. The question is, What can we do to stop that war? What can we do to stop the people who, in the name of America, are killing babies, women, and children? We have to say to ourselves that there's a higher law than the law of a fool named Rusk; there's a higher law than the law of a buffoon named Johnson. It's the law of each of us. We will not murder anybody who they say kill, and if we decide to kill, *we're* going to decide who it shall be. This country will only stop the war in Vietnam when the young men who are made to fight it begin to say, "Hell, no, we ain't going."

The peace movement has been a failure because it hasn't gotten off the college campuses where everybody has a 2S and is not afraid of being drafted anyway. The problem is how you can move out of that into the white ghettos of this country and articulate a position for those white youth who do not want to go. You cannot do that. It is sometimes ironic that many of the peace groups have begun to call SNCC violent and say they can no longer support us, when we are in fact the most militant organization for peace or civil rights or human rights against the war in Vietnam in this country today. There isn't one organization that has begun to meet our stand on the war in Vietnam. We not only say we are against the war in Vietnam; we are against the draft. No man has the right to take a man for two years and train him to be a killer. Any black man fighting in the war in Vietnam is nothing but a black mercenary. Any time a black man leaves the country where he can't vote to supposedly deliver the vote to somebody else, he's a black mercenary. Any time a black man leaves this country, gets shot in Vietnam on foreign ground, and returns home and you won't give him a burial place in his own homeland, he's a black mercenary. Even if I believed the lies of Johnson, that we're fighting to give democracy to the people in Vietnam, as a black man living in this country I wouldn't fight to give this to anybody. We have to use our bodies and our minds in the only way that we see fit. We must begin, as the philosopher Camus says, to come alive by say-

ing "No." This country is a nation of thieves. It stole everything it has, beginning with black people. The U.S. cannot
justify its existence as the policeman of the world any
longer. The marines are at ready disposal to bring democracy, and if the Vietnamese don't want democracy, well
then, "We'll just wipe them out, because they don't deserve
to live if they won't have our way of life."

There is a more immediate question: What do you do on
your campus? Do you raise questions about the hundred
black students who were kicked off campus a couple of
weeks ago? Eight hundred? And how does that question
begin to move? Do you begin to relate to people outside the
ivory tower and university walls? Do you think you're
capable of building those human relationships as the
country now stands? You're fooling yourself. It is impossible for white and black people to talk about building a
relationship based on humanity when the country is the
way it is, when the institutions are clearly against us.

We have found all the myths of the country to be nothing but downright lies. We were told that if we worked
hard we would succeed, and if that were true we would
own this country lock, stock, and barrel. We have picked
the cotton for nothing; we are the maids in the kitchens
of liberal white people; we are the janitors, the porters,
the elevator men; we sweep up your college floors. We
are the hardest workers and the lowest paid. It is nonsensical for people to talk about human relationships until
they are willing to build new institutions. Black people
are economically insecure. White liberals are economically
secure. Can you begin to build an economic coalition? Are
the liberals willing to share their salaries with the economically insecure black people they so much love? Then
if you're not, are you willing to start building new institutions that will provide economic security for black
people? That's the question *we* want to deal with!

American students are perhaps the most politically
unsophisticated students in the world. Across every coun-

try of the world, while we were growing up, students were leading the major revolutions of their countries. We have not been able to do that. They have been politically aware of their existence. In South America our neighbors have one every 24 hours just to remind us that they are politically aware. But we have been unable to grasp it because we've always moved in the field of morality and love while people have been politically jiving with our lives. You can't move morally against men like Brown and Reagan. You can't move morally against Lyndon Baines Johnson because he is an immoral man. He doesn't know what it's all about. So you've got to move politically. We have to develop a political sophistication that doesn't parrot ("The two-party system is the best system in the world"). We have to raise questions about whether we need new types of political institutions in this country, and we in SNCC maintain that we need them now. Any time Lyndon Baines Johnson can head a party that has in it Bobby Kennedy, Wayne Morse, Eastland, Wallace, and all those other supposed-to-be-liberal cats, there's something wrong with that party. They're moving politically, not morally. If that party refuses to seat black people from Mississippi and goes ahead and seats racists like Eastland and his clique, it's clear to me that they're moving politically, and that one cannot begin to talk morality to people like that.

We must question the values of this society, and I maintain that black people are the best people to do that since we have been excluded from that society. We ought to think whether or not we want to become a part of that society. That's precisely what the Student Nonviolent Coordinating Committee is doing. We are raising questions about this country. I do not want to be a part of the American pie. The American pie means raping South Africa, beating Vietnam, beating South America, raping the Philippines, raping every country you've been in. I don't want any of your blood money. I don't want to be part of that system. We are the generation who has found this country to be a world power and the wealthiest country in the world. We must question whether or not we want this country to continue being the wealthiest country in the world at the price of raping everybody else. And because black people are saying we do not now want to become a part of you, we are called reverse racists. Ain't that a gas?

White society has caused the failure of nonviolence. I was always surprised at Quakers who came to Alabama and counseled me to be nonviolent, but didn't have the guts to tell James Clark to be nonviolent. That's where nonviolence needs to be preached—to Jim Clark, not to black people. White people should conduct their nonviolent schools in Cicero where they are needed, not among black people in Mississippi. Six-foot-two men kick little black children in Grenada—can you conduct nonviolent schools there? Can you name one black man today who has killed anybody white and is still alive? Even after a rebellion, when some black brothers throw bricks and bottles, ten thousand of them have to pay the price. When the white policeman comes in, anybody who's black is arrested because we all look alike.

The youth of this country must begin to raise those questions. We are going to have to change the foreign policy of this country. One of the problems with the peace movement is that it is too caught up in Vietnam, and if America pulled out the troops from Vietnam this week, next week you'd have to get another peace movement for Santo Domingo. *We have to hook up with black people around the world; and that hookup must not only be psychological, but real.* If South America were to rebel today, and black people were to shoot the hell out of all the white people there, as they should, Standard Oil would crumble tomorrow. If South Africa were to go today, Chase Manhattan Bank would crumble tomorrow. If Zimbabwe, which is called Rhodesia by white people, were to go tomorrow, General Electric would cave in on the East Coast. How do we stop those institutions that are so willing to fight against "Communist aggression" but close their eyes against racist oppression? We're not talking about a policy of aid or sending Peace Corps people in to teach people how to read and write and build houses while we steal their raw materials from them. Because that's all this country does. What underdeveloped countries need is information about how to become industrialized, so they can keep their raw materials where they have them, produce goods, sell them to this country for the price it's supposed to pay. Instead, America keeps selling goods back to them for a profit and keeps sending our modern-day missionaries there, calling them the sons of Kennedy. And if the youth are going to participate in that program, how do you begin to control the Peace Corps?

This country assumes that if someone is poor, they are poor because of their own individual blight, or because they weren't born on the right side of town, or they had too many children, or went in the army too early, or because their father was a drunk, or they didn't care about school—they made a mistake. That's a lot of nonsense. Poverty is well calculated in this country, and the reason why the poverty program won't work is because the calculators of poverty are administering it.

How can you, as the youth in this country, move to start carrying those things out? Move into the white community. We have developed a movement in the black community. The white activist has miserably failed to develop the movement inside of his community. Will white people have the courage to go into white communities and start organizing them? That's the question for the white activist. We won't get caught up in questions about power. This country knows what power is. It knows what Black Power is because it deprived black people of it for over four hundred years. White people associate Black Power with violence because of their own inabilty to deal with blackness. If we had said "Negro power" nobody would get scared. Everybody would support it. If we said power for colored people, everybody'd be for that, but it is the word "black" that bothers people in this country, and that's their problem, not mine. That's the lie that says anything black is bad.

You're all a college and university crowd. You've taken your basic logic course. You know about major premise, minor premise. People have been telling you anything all black is bad. Let's make that our major premise.

Major premise: Anything all black is bad.

Minor premise or particular premise: I am all black.

Therefore . . . I'm never going to be put in that bag; I'm all black and I'm all good. Anything all black is not necessarily bad. Anything all black is only bad when you use force to keep whites out. Now that's what white people have done in this country, and they're projecting their same fears and guilt on us, and we won't have it. Let them handle their own affairs and their own guilt. Let them find their own psychologists. We refuse to be the therapy for white society any longer. We have gone stark, raving mad trying to do it.

I look at Dr. King on television every single day, and I say to myself: "Now there is a man who's desperately needed in this country. There is a man full of love. There is a man full of mercy. There is a man full of compassion." But every time I see Lyndon on television, I say, "Martin, baby, you got a long way to go."

If we were to be real and honest, we would have to admit that most people in this country see things black and white. We live in a country that's geared that way. White people would have to admit that they are afraid to go into a black ghetto at night. They're afraid because they'd be "beat up," "lynched," "looted," "cut up," etc. It happens to black people inside the ghetto every day, incidentally. Since white people are afraid of that, they get a man to do it for them—a policeman. Figure his mentality. The first time a black man jumps, that white man's going to shoot him. Police brutality is going to exist on that level. The only time I hear people talk about nonviolence is when black people move to defend themselves against white people. Black people cut themselves every night in the ghetto—nobody talks about nonviolence. Lyndon Baines Johnson is busy bombing the hell out of Vietnam—nobody talks about nonviolence. White people beat up black people every day—nobody talks about nonviolence. But as soon as black people start to move, the double standard comes into being. You can't defend yourself. You show me a black man who advocates aggressive violence who would be able to live in this country. Show him to me. Isn't it hypocritical for Lyndon to talk about how you can't accomplish anything by looting and you must accomplish it by the legal ways? What does he know about legality? Ask Ho Chi Minh.

We must wage a psychological battle on the right for black people to define themselves as they see fit, and organize themselves as they see fit. We don't know whether the white community will allow for that organizing, because once they do they must also allow for the organizing inside their own community. It doesn't make a difference, though—we're going to organize our way. The question is how we're going to facilitate those matters, whether it's going to be done with a thousand policemen with submachine guns, or whether it's going to be done in a context where it's allowed by white people warding off those policemen. Are white people who call themselves activists ready to move into the white communities on two counts, on building new political institutions to destroy the old ones that we have, and to move around the concept of white youth refusing to go into the army? If so, than we can start to build a new world. We must urge you to fight now to be the leaders of today, not tomorrow. This country is a nation of thieves. It stands on the brink of becoming a nation of murderers. We must stop it. We must stop it. We must stop it.

We are on the move for our liberation. We're tired of trying to prove things to white people. We are tired of trying to explain to white people that we're not going to hurt them. We are concerned with getting the things we want, the things we have to have to be able to function. The question is, Will white people overcome their racism and allow for that to happen in this country? If not, we have no choice but to say very clearly, "Move on over, or we're going to move on over you."

6

At
Morgan
State

It's good to be back here at Morgan. I used to party here when I was at school—after we sat-in in Baltimore on Route 40.

I hope some of the people who have been disagreeing with the concept of Black Power are here. I would suggest they read two articles—one that I wrote for the *New York Review of Books* in September [1966] and one that appeared in the *Massachusetts Review* in 1966.*

They explain the theoretical concept of Black Power;

Morgan State College, Baltimore, January 28, 1967.
* Included in this collection.

they criticize the exponents of the coalition theory and those who say that integration is the only route to solving the racial problem in this country.

I would think that at a black university it would be absurd for me to talk about Black Power, that rather I should talk to black students about what their role is to be in the coming struggle. And so my remarks today are addressed to you, black students of Morgan, to give you a chance to hear some of the things that you never hear about, your need to stop being ashamed of being black and come on home. Though there are many members of the press here, you should pay them no mind because they will not be able to understand what we are talking about.

When I was supposed to speak at this university in October, they canceled the speech. Now I understand there were all sorts of bureaucratic tieups for canceling the speech. We know that elections were close at hand in Maryland and there was a feeling—on my part, I am not saying that anyone really said this—that the people were scared, and so they canceled the speech. They were scared that if I spoke here on the "your house is your castle" concept, Mahoney would win.* One of the reasons I want to talk about that is that I think it is important to understand what that means. What I think the country is trying to do is to kill the free speech of the Student Nonviolent Coordinating Committee.

I'd like to read from one of my favorite men, Frederick Douglass—I hope he is yours. You know Baltimore was his home spot, where he spent his early age. It was from Baltimore that he escaped to freedom.

I want to read it because I think it is crystal clear in our minds what we must do in this generation to move for Black Power. Our mothers scrubbed floors. Our fathers were Uncle Toms. They didn't do that so we could scrub

* An avid segregationist, George Mahoney ran against Spiro Agnew for governorship of Maryland. His campaign slogan on the issue of integrated housing was "A Man's Home Is His Castle."

floors and be Uncle Toms. They did it so that this generation can fight for Black Power—and that is what we are
about to do and that is what you ought to understand.

Mr. Douglass said:

> Those who profess to favor freedom, yet deprecate
> agitation, are men who want crops without plow-
> ing up the ground; they want rain without thun-
> der and lightning; they want the ocean without the
> awful roar of its many waters.
>
> Power concedes nothing without demands—it
> never did and it never will. Find out just what
> any people will submit to and you have found out
> the exact amount of injustice and wrong which
> will be imposed upon them; and these will con-
> tinue till they have resisted with either words or
> blows or with both. The limits of tyrants are pre-
> scribed by the endurance of those whom they sup-
> press.

Following in Mr. Douglass's footsteps we intend to
strike our first blow for our liberation, and we will let the
chips fall where they may. We do not wish to earn the
good will of anybody who is oppressing us. They should
rather try to earn our good will, since they have been
oppressing us.

This country has been able to make us ashamed of
being black. One of the first recognitions of a free people
is that we must be united as a people; we must understand the concept of peoplehood and not be ashamed of
ourselves. We must stop imitating white society and begin
to create for ourselves and our own and begin to embody
our own cultural patterns so that we will be holding to
those things that we have created, and holding them
dear.

For example: it is nonsensical for black people to have
debutante balls. It is nonsensical because you are imita-

ting that which white society has given to you and that which you know nothing about. Your fathers slaved for one year to save $500 so that you can walk up in some white dress for one night talking about virginity. Wouldn't it be better to take that $500 and give it to Morgan so that you could begin to develop a good black institution?

Imitation runs deep in the black community in this country. It runs very deep. You know, when we first got people to go to college and they went to the first white university in this country, there were things called fraternities and sororities. Our black brothers and sisters could not get into these fraternities. They were kept out because of the color of their skin. So what did our brothers do? They turned around and formed something called Alphas, and only light-skinned Negroes could get in. Our black sisters, not to be outdone, formed AKA, for bluebloods only. The other dark-skinned brothers, not to be outdone, set up Omega and Kappa. And then, of course, we had the counterparts, the Deltas.

Now, wouldn't it have been far better if those people, instead of imitating a society that had been built on excluding them, had turned around and built a fraternity that included everybody, light-skinned and dark-skinned?

Perhaps that is the greatest problem you, as black students, face: you are never asked to create, only to imitate.

Then we come to the question of definitions. It is very, very important, because people who can define are the masters. Understand that. You remember a couple of years ago when our black leaders would talk about integration. They would say we want to integrate. They would be talking about good houses, good schools, good neighborhoods. White people would say, You want to marry my daughter. They would say, No, I don't want to marry your daughter; we just want to be your brother, we don't want to be your brother-in-law. Or: We want to live next door to you, we don't want to live in your bedroom. What the white people were doing was defining integration for those black leaders, and those black leaders allowed them to. By the time those cats finished reacting to a definition by a white man, they were out the window. And by the time they came back to being aggressive the black community said later for those cats. They allowed white people to define their reaction.

Now when we get asked that question in SNCC you know what we say: Your daughter, your sister, and your mama. The white woman is not the queen of the world, she is not the Virgin Mary, she can be made like any other woman. Let's move on, let's move on.

They try the same things now. These days, I say Black Power and someone says, you mean violence. And they expect me to say, No, no, I don't mean violence, I don't mean that. Later for you, I am master of my own term. If Black Power means violence to you, that is your problem, as is marrying your daughter.

I know what it means in my mind. I will stand clear. And you must understand that, because the first need of a free people is to be able to define their own terms and have those terms recognized by their oppressors. It is also the first need that all oppressors must suppress. I think it is what Camus talks about. He says that when a slave says no, he begins to exist. You see you define to contain. That's all you do. If we allow white people to define us by calling us Negroes, which means apathetic, lazy, stupid, and all those other things, then we accept those definitions.

We must define what we are—and then move from our definitions and tell them, Recognize what we say we are!

We all watch cowboy movies all the time. You know, there would be a fight and there would be Indians and they would be coming from the hills and Chief Crazy Horse would have a million Indians and they would be yelling, "Wha, wha, wha," and they would be killing the good white women. And at last here comes the cavalry. They would come riding in and they would get out their guns and shoot up everybody—men, forward march, forward, shoot. Look out, that one on the right. Boom, we've got him, he's dead. They would come back and they would say, we had a victory today. We killed the Indians.

The next time the Indians would win; they would beat the hell out of the cavalry and the white man would come back and say, Those dirty Indians, they massacred us.

See what they were doing. They were putting connotations in our minds. A massacre is not as good as a victory because in a victory you shoot people and you kill them in an honorable way, but in a massacre you kill with a knife and everybody knows that's foul.

But the Indians had victories too. That we must begin to recognize. That's very important.

You ever listen to the news? Every day now, Viet Cong terrorists bomb and kill fifty women and children, what a shame. In the meantime, United States jet bombers have been flying heavily over Hanoi, dropping bombs.

The power to define is the most important power that we have. It is he who is master who can define; that was cleared in the McCarthy period. If McCarthy said you were a communist, you had to get up and say, No I am not a communist. Who the hell is McCarthy? I mean who is he? He had the power to define. It is the same thing. "My fellow Americans, the communists, the slanted-eye Viet Cong are our enemy. You must go kill them." You don't have the right to define whether or not that cat is your enemy. The master has defined it for you. And when he says "jump," you say, "how high, boss?" We must begin to define our own terms and certainly our own concept of ourselves and let those who are not capable of following us fall by the wayside.

You must begin to understand the nature of this country called America, which exploits all other, non-white countries. You know what they are talking about—you see that's the thing with definitions—you know, we are fighting for freedom, democracy, for peace. Nobody questions it. Yes, we are going to kill for freedom, democracy, and peace. These little Chinese, Vietnamese yellow people haven't got sense enough to know they want their democracy, but we are going to fight for them. We'll give it to them because Santa Claus is still alive.

I want to read a quote made August 4, 1953, before the United States Governors' Convention in Seattle. Incidentally, I highly recommend this book. It is *Vietnam, Vietnam,* by Felix Green.

I think the trouble with our black students is that they just don't read enough. If we could get books like we could boogaloo we would be uptight.

"Now let us assume," the quote says, "that we lost Indochina . . ." Now that is in 1953, the U.S. was not fighting the war, the French were fighting it for the United States. America was just giving them the money.

Now let us assume that we lost Indochina, the tin and tungsten that we so greatly value from that area would cease coming. So when the United States votes $400 million to help that war, we are not voting a give-away program. We are voting for the cheapest way that we can to prevent the occurrence of something that would be of a most terrible significance to the United States of America, our security, our power and ability to get certain things we need from the riches of the Indo-Chinese territory and from Southeast Asia.

That quote was made by President Dwight D. Eisenhower—now we may say that Dwight wasn't too smart. But that was in 1953. So, well, we figure, you know Dwight wasn't too smart and that was a long time ago and we have become more civilized.

I want to read you a statement now by Henry Cabot

Lodge. He's the good-looking one, you know—tall, blond hair, blue eyes. He said, a year ago:

> Geographically, Vietnam stands at the hub of a vast area of the world—Southeast Asia—an area with a population of 249 million persons. . . . He who holds or has influence in Vietnam can affect the future of the Philippines and Formosa to the east, Thailand and Burma with their huge rice surpluses to the west, and Malaysia and Indonesia with their rubber, ore and tin to the south. . . . Vietnam thus does not exist in a geographical vacuum—from it large storehouses of wealth and population can be influenced and undermined.

He is absolutely right. That's what that war is all about. And that's why we are not going.

Those are the words of the ambassador to Saigon, they are not my words. And he outlines very clearly what the war is being fought for.

If you understand anything about this country, you know that 75 per cent of the budget is spent on war materials. That means that for this country to survive it must always be at war.

You will not get a victory for this country if you win in Vietnam. That's no victory. The country must keep fighting. You do not invent things that have no use. You invent them so that they have a use. And every time you invent a better bomb, you must drop it. So you invent another bomb. That is why this country keeps going at the breakneck speed it is going in terms of its military might. We are told that it is civilized—another word to define.

You know Rudyard Kipling defined civilization for us. He talked about the white man's burden. Pick up your whiteness and go to Africa to cultivate the savages and illiterates. So all these nice, white people of good will who wanted to do well, they got in their little black robes and they went to Africa and they saw these little black savage women, man, running around with no shirts on. "Why, you dirty thing, cover yourself up." Africans were never excited, so it must have been the nice, white people who were excited because they wanted them to cover it up. Africans didn't even know what breasts were for except to feed their young.

But the white people brought their concepts. When they left they had the land and we had their religion. And that was civilization for them. Indeed, what is civilization? To be able to drop bombs on Hiroshima? To be able to drop bombs on Hanoi? Is that civilization? Do we want to be civilized too?

This country has said that civilization is at stake and there is no other solution but war. So what they do is train us in ROTC. You dig it? All they do in ROTC is teach you how to kill. You may try to justify it all you want, but your job is to kill. The job of the army is to kill. ROTC doesn't teach you how to become anything. If you want me to be taught something, build a school in my neighborhood and let me go there. Don't tell me about going to Vietnam to learn anything.

I have to be appalled at the president of the university who stands up and says that Black Power is about violence while at this very campus he encourages institutionalized violence—compulsory ROTC—and does not speak about that. Who does he think he is kidding? There is nothing wrong with violence. It is just who is able to control it. That's what counts. Everybody knows that. You have institutionalized violence on your campus. You have to dress up in a monkey suit and train how to kill once a week. And what is your response to that as black students, coming to a university where they are supposed to teach you civilization? Is that civilization too? That one must kill?

Is that what you are imitating? Is it for you not to reason why at a university, but to do and die? Do you not have the guts to say: Hell, no. Do you not have the guts to say, I will not allow anyone to make me a hired killer.

When I decide to kill, since it is the greatest crime that man can commit, I alone will make that decision, and I will decide whom to kill.

You are now at a vast black university where they have already incorporated violence in your thinking. And here you are marching around every Friday, or Thursday, or Wednesday or whatever it is, with your shoes spit-shined, until three o'clock in the morning—marching with a gun in your hand, learning all about how to shoot.

And somebody talks about violence. No, I am not violent, I don't believe in violence. I don't want no Black Power. I ain't got nothing to do with violence. Over in Vietnam they put you on a front line and you are shooting. But that is not violence because you can't define for yourself. You ought to tell the school that if you wanted to learn how to kill you would have gone to West Point. You came here to learn how to help your people of Baltimore in the ghettos, and then you turn your backs on them as soon as you get a chance.

What can you tell a black man who lives in the ghettos in Baltimore about killing? Hasn't he been subjected to it all of his life? What is your analysis about the rebellions that have been occurring all around the state?

Are you like everybody else? Are you against violence? Do you analyze? Do you recognize what it means?

The reason they say that we preach violence isn't because we preach violence, but because we refuse to condemn black people who throw rocks and bottles at policemen. That is why. And I say that is the only reason why. Look at all the other Negro leaders—so-called leaders— every time there is a riot:

We deplore violence, we avoid use of violence, it is very, very bad, there is only a small group of

70

vagabonds, they don't represent our community, and violence never accomplishes anything. Yes, we are training our boys to go to Vietnam. We think it is a good thing to send them to Vietnam, but violence never accomplishes anything at all.

Now, you have got to understand this very clearly. If you know anything about the ghetto, you know that on any given Friday or Saturday night there is more violence inside the ghetto than anyplace else in any given city. You know that we cut and butcher and shoot each other. And do you also know that in any given ghetto there is more police power, that is, in terms of numbers, there are more police per block, per square inch, than in any other area of the city? What does that mean to you? On Friday night while there are more police, there is still more violence among black people. Obviously they don't give a damn about the violence among black people.

What it points out is the problem between property rights and human rights in this country—a problem the country is not capable of facing up to. Let one black boy throw one rock at some filthy grocery store and the whole damned National Guard comes into our ghetto. Property rights mean more than human rights and we in the ghetto do not own the property. If we get robbed, you can call the policemen till you turn white. He ain't coming. You know it as well as I do. But just hit a grocery store, just throw a Molotov cocktail through a window and see how quick they come in. They deplore violence.

It's all right with them when we cut each other in the street on Friday and Saturday nights. We need non-violence in the black community, that's where we need it. We have to learn to love and respect ourselves. That's where it should begin. That is where it must begin. Because if *we* don't love us, ain't nobody going to love us.

The people who have power in our ghettos are the property owners and when their stores are touched they call the National Guard.

But analyze that one step further. Everybody in our ghettos knows that we are charged higher prices for rotten meat. Everybody knows that, but nobody says, We deplore the high prices they charge the Negro for rotten meat. Nobody moves to readjust the problems black people are facing in the ghetto like the slumlord. And if they try, they would find out that the people who own the property are the people who make the laws.

Property rights, that's what the United States Constitution is based on. You should know that. You are three-fifths of a man until this very day. Property rights. People who didn't own property could not vote when this country was first founded, not until years afterwards. So the analysis is the question of property versus property-less people.

That's what those rebellions are about, nothing else, nothing less. And what appalls me about the black leaders is they do not have the guts to condemn the grocery store owner. Anytime a man has been charging us all that money for fifteen years, his store should have been bombed five years ago. It should have been out of the neighborhood five years ago. And if nobody wants to do it, then you can't blame people when they move to do it for themselves.

If you want to stop rebellion, then eradicate the cause.

It is time for you to stop running away from being black. You are college students, you should think. It is time for you to begin to understand that you, as the growing intellectuals, the black intellectuals of this country, must begin to define beauty for black people.

Beauty in this society is defined by someone with a narrow nose, thin lips, white skin. You ain't got none of that. If your lips are thick, bite them in. Hold your nose;

don't drink coffee because it makes you black. Everybody knows black is bad. Can you begin to get the guts to develop criteria for beauty for black people? Your nose is boss, your lips are thick, you are black, and you are beautiful. Can you begin to do it so that you are not ashamed of your hair and you don't cut it to the scalp so that naps won't show?

Girls, are you ready? Obviously it is your responsibility to begin to define the criteria for black people concerning their beauty. You are running around with your Nadinola cream. The black campuses of this country are becoming infested with wigs and Mustangs and you are to blame for it. You are to blame for it. What is your responsibility to your fellow black brothers? Why are you here? So that you can become a social worker or so that you can kick down a door in the middle of the night to look for a pair of shoes?

Is that what you come to college for? So that you can keep the kid in the ghetto school, so that you can ride up in a big Bonneville with an AKA sign stuck on the back? Is that your responsibility? What is your responsibility to black people of Baltimore who are hungry for the knowledge you are supposed to have?

Is it so that you can just get over? Do you forget that it is their sweat that put you where you are? Do you not know that your black mothers scrubbed floors so you can get here—and the minute you get out, you turn your back on them? What is your responsibility, black students? What is it? Is it to become a teacher so you can be programmed into a ghetto school? So that you can get up and say, "It's a shame how our children are culturally deprived"?

What do you know about culturally deprived? What is your definition of culture? Is it not anything man-made? How the hell can I be culturally deprived? You deny my very existence, to use that term.

Do you question what they tell you at school? Or do you only accept, carry it back, get over, go out to further stymie black people in the ghetto?

I blame you for the rebellions across the country this summer. And I will blame you again when they increase this summer. It is your obligation to be back in the ghetto helping out black people who are looking, who are acting, begging, and thinking a way to solve their problems. And you are running out of the ghetto as fast as your sports cars and Mustangs can carry you.

What is your responsibility, black students of Morgan? Do you know about Du Bois? Have you read Douglass? Do you know Richard Wright? Can you quote J. A. Rogers? Do you know Claude McKay?

Can you understand, can you understand LeRoi Jones? There is a young man with me now. His name is Eldridge Cleaver. He just spent eight years in jail. He is writing some of the most profound writing that has come out in the country from black men. Do you know him? Have you read his stuff? Why haven't you read his stuff? Is it because you are too busy trying to find out where the Kappas are partying Friday night?

Why is it that you haven't read his stuff? Is it that you are spit-shining your shoes so that you can become a lieutenant colonel to go to Vietnam when you graduate?

Why is it that you haven't read his stuff? Is it that you don't want to read anything about being black because you, too, are ashamed of it and are running from it? So you want to run to your debutante ball. So you want to run to your Kappa fraternity ball and forget all else.

When the ghettos rebel you are going to be the buffer, and you are the ones who are going to be caught in the middle. The gate is swinging open. Brothers and sisters, you had better come home early this summer. You had better take what knowledge you have and use it to benefit black people in the ghetto.

You had better recognize that individualism is a luxury that black students can no longer afford. You had better begin to see yourself as a people and as a group and, therefore, you need to help to advance that group.

Can you be aggressive? Can you say that Baltimore is almost 52 per cent black, and black people should own it, run it, lock stock and barrel? Or are you afraid?

Can you not go out and organize those people to take the political power that they have been denied and by which they've been oppressed and exploited? Can you not help? Are you too busy trying to be a doctor and lawyer so that you can get a big car and a big house and talk about your house in the suburbs. Am I the only one out there?

Can you begin to say that James Brown is us, that he is a musical genius as much as Bach or Beethoven? Can you understand your culture? Can you make them teach it to you here in college, rather than teach you Bach and Beethoven, which is only one-sided? Why can't you also have James Brown so that you can begin to know what culture is all about?

I want to finish with one quote—actually there are two quotes I want to finish with.

I want to read it because I don't want to make a mistake. The quote I want to read before I close is from Bertrand Russell. You know about the war tribunal. You should. Bertrand Russell is calling the war tribunals to judge the leaders of this country for their actions in Vietnam. I have been asked to serve on it and I am greatly honored. I want to read a quote he calls "An Appeal to My Conscience." The war in Vietnam should have interest for you not only personally, but also because it is very political for black people. When McNamara says he is going to draft 30 per cent of the black people out of the ghettos, baby, that is nothing but urban removal. You should realize you are going to be the fellows leading the charges of your black people. Do you have the guts to stand up now and say I will not follow law and order, I will follow my own conscience. That's what they sent Eichmann to jail for, you know, because he followed law and order.

The choices are very clear. You either suffer or you inflict suffering. Either you go to the Leavenworth federal penitentiary in Kansas or you become a killer. I will choose to suffer. I will go to jail. To hell with this country.

Mr. Russell:

> Just as in the case of Spain, Vietnam is a barbarous rehearsal. It is our intention that neither the bona fides nor the authenticity of this tribunal will be susceptible to challenge from those who have so much to hide.
>
> President Johnson, Dean Rusk, Robert McNamara, Henry Cabot Lodge, General Westmoreland and their fellow criminals will be brought before a wider justice than they recognize and a more profound condemnation than they are equipped to understand.

That is a profound statement.

The last statement that I want to leave you with is by John Donne. He said the "death of any man diminishes me because I am involved in mankind."

This generation is not involved in mankind. When we began to crawl, they sent six million people to an oven and we blinked our eyes. When we walked, they sent our uncles to Korea. And we grew up in a cold war. We, this generation, must save the world. We must become involved in mankind. We must not allow them the chance to kill everything and anything that gets in their way. We must not become part of the machine.

I want to read my favorite quotation to conclude.

"If I am not for myself, who will be? If I am for myself alone, who am I? If not now, when? And if not you, who?"

7

The Dialectics of Liberation

I had intended to prepare a written speech for the Dialectics, and had started to prepare it three weeks before the trip, but the United States government thought that as I was starving it would be better if they saw to it that I got some meals every day, so they confined me to their prison system, and I lost all the notes. So I've been trying to get another one together.

Now since I've been at the Congress I've been very confused, because I'm not a psychologist or a psychiatrist, I'm a political activist. I don't deal with the individual, I

Congress on the Dialectics of Liberation, London, July 18, 1967.

think it's a cop-out when people talk about the individual. What we're talking about around the United States today, and I believe around the Third World, is the system of international white supremacy coupled with international capitalism. We're out to smash that system. People who see themselves as part of that system are going to be smashed with it—or we're going to be smashed.

So I'm not going to talk about the individual. For one thing it will be seen that the black man's alienation is not an individual question, it is a question of socio-diagnostics. The Negro problem does not resolve itself into the problem of individual Negroes living among white men, but rather of Negroes as a class that is exploited, enslaved, and despised by the colonialist, capitalist society, which is only accidentally white. But since it is accidentally white, that's what we talk about—white Western society.

The other reason why I won't talk about the individual is that whenever you raise questions about racial problems to white Western society, each white man says: "Well, don't blame me, I'm only one person and I really don't feel that way. Actually I have nothing against you, I see you as an equal. You're just as good as I am—almost." I want to clear that up—to point out the difference between individual racism and institutionalized racism.

The first type, individual racism, consists of overt acts by individuals, and usually the immediate result is the death of the victim, or the traumatic and violent destruction of property. This type can be recorded on T.V. cameras and can frequently be observed in the process.

The second type is less overt, far more subtle, less identifiable in terms of specific individuals committing the acts, but it is no less destructive of human life. It's part of the overall operation of established and respected forces in the society, so it doesn't receive the condemnation that the first type does.

Let me give you an example of the first type. When unidentified white terrorists bomb a black church and kill five black children, that is an act of individual racism, widely deplored by most segments of the world. But when in that same city, Birmingham, Alabama, not five but five hundred black babies die each year because of lack of proper food, shelter and medical facilities, and thousands more are destroyed and maimed physically, emotionally and intellectually because of conditions of poverty and discrimination in the black community, that is a function of institutionalized racism. When a black family moves into a home in a white neighborhood, and it is stoned, burned or routed out, the latter is an overt act of individual racism, and many people condemn that, at least in words. But it is institutionalized racism that keeps the black people locked in dilapidated slums, tenements, where they must live out their daily lives subject to the prey of exploitative slum landlords, merchants, loan sharks and the restrictive practices of real-estate agents. We're talking now about the U.S., but I think you can apply a little of it to London. But the society either pretends it does not know of institutionalized racism, or is incapable of doing anything meaningful about the conditions of institutionalized racism. And the resistance to doing anything meaningful about institutionalized racism stems from the fact that Western society enjoys its luxury from institutionalized racism, and therefore, were it to end institutionalized racism, it would in fact destroy itself.

One of the major tools of racism is mystification, so I want to get into the idea of demystifying human beings, and I'm talking about the Third World, I'm not talking about the white West. I think that the Third World are the people who, at least in the United States, black people are concerned with; the white West has been able to do very well for itself. I want to talk, then, very specifically about a number of things under demystification.

The first is the importance of definitions. Second, cultural integrity versus cultural imposition. And then I want to talk about the United States, specifically the cities and the rebellions—"riots," they're called by the white press—that are occurring in the United States which are going to lead to guerrilla warfare. And I want to talk about violence because the West is always upset by violence when a black man uses it. Yeah.

In one of my favorite books, *Alice in Wonderland*, there's a debate between Humpty Dumpty and Alice around the question of definitions:

"When I use a word," Humpty Dumpty said, in a rather scornful tone, "it means just what I choose it to mean. Neither more nor less."

"The question is," said Alice, "whether you can make words mean so many different things."

"The question is," said Humpty Dumpty, "who is to be master. That is all."

And I think Lewis Carroll is right: those who can define are the masters. White Western society has been able to define, and that's why she has been the master. The white youth of my generation in the West today starts off with subconscious racism because he accepts the writings of the West, which have either destroyed, distorted, lied about history. He starts off with a basic assumption of superiority that he doesn't even recognize.

The people of the Third World are going to have to stop accepting the definitions imposed upon them by the West. Frederick Douglass, the great black leader of the 1800s, said that slave seeks his liberation when, and only when, he stops obeying a master. Camus said the same thing one hundred years later on the first page of *The Rebel:* when a slave stops accepting definitions imposed upon him by his master, then, and only then, he begins to move and create a life.

History books tell you that nothing happens until a white man comes along. "Who discovered America?"

"Christopher Columbus." "Who discovered China?" "Marco Polo." I used to be told in the West Indies that I was not discovered until Sir Walter Raleigh needed supplies for his ship, and then he came along and found me and said "Whup! I have discovered you!" and my history began.

But let us examine the racism in that statement—let us examine it very closely. Columbus did not discover America. Columbus may be the first recorded white man to set foot on America—that is all. There were people there before Columbus. But white Western society never recognizes the existence of non-white people, either consciously or subconsciously, so that all around the world, the peoples of the Third World never did anything until some white man came along. And that's why China's nonexistent, because Mao won't let no white folk in there. Yeah. And pretty soon Hong Kong is going to be nonexistent, because they're going to kick them out.

All through history classes we were studying "Western civilization," and that meant that all else was uncivilized. One of the biggest lies that Western society could have done was to name itself Western civilization. White kids who read that today never recognize that they're being told that they are superior to everybody else because they have produced civilization. At best, it's a misnomer; at worst, and more correctly, it's a damn lie. Western "civilization" has been, as a matter of fact, most barbaric. We are told that Western civilization begins with the Greeks, and the epitome of that civilization is Alexander the Great. The only thing I remember about Alexander the Great was that at age twenty-six he wept because there were no more people to murder and rob. That is the epitome of Western civilization. And if you're not satisfied with that, you could always take the Roman Empire: their favorite pastimes were watching men kill each other or lions eating up men—they were a civilized people. The fact is that their civilization, as they called it, stemmed

81

from their oppression of other peoples, which allowed them a certain luxury, at the expense of those other people. That exploitation for luxury has been interpreted as "civilization" for the West, and that exploitation for luxury is precisely what it has done. The only difference is that after the Roman Empire, when the British Empire—on which the sun never used to set, but today it sets, sometimes it don't even rise—began to exploit other peoples, what they did was they let color be the sole criterion in choosing which peoples they would exploit.

You've been able to lie about terms, so you've been able to call people like Cecil Rhodes a philanthropist when in fact he was a murderer, a rapist, a plunderer, and a thief. But you call Cecil Rhodes a philanthropist because, after he stole our diamonds and our gold, then he gave us some crumbs so we can go to school and become just like you. And that was called philanthropy. But we are renaming it: the place is not called Rhodesia any more, it is called Zimbabwe—that's its proper name. And Cecil Rhodes is not called a philanthropist any more, he's known to be a thief. You can keep your Rhodes Scholars, we don't want the money that came from the sweat of our people.

I'm always appalled when some white person tells me that "progress is being made." I always ask him, "Progress for whom and from whom?" Progress for white people might be made, because I would say that since World War II they have learned a little how to get around, to get along with people of color. But I don't think there's been progress for the black people, there's not been progress for the people of color around the Third World. And progress will not be measured for us by white people. We will have to tell you when progress is being made. You cannot tell us when progress is being made, because progress for us is getting you off our backs, and that's the only progress that we can see.

There have been a lot of changes but no progress.

When I was a young man in the West Indies, I had to

read Rudyard Kipling's *The White Man's Burden*. I thought the best thing white men could do for me was to leave me alone, but Rudyard Kipling said they should come and save me because I was half savage, half child. It was very white of him. Because the white West felt somehow that it was better than everybody else, it has used force to impose its culture on the Third World wherever it has been. If a few settlers left England to go to Zimbabwe, there was no reason for them to rename that country Rhodesia, after themselves, and then force everybody to speak their language. If they'd had respect for the cultures of other people, they would have spoken the language of those people and adopted their religions. But the West was powerful—that's the word nobody wants to talk about, power. It was only power that made people bow their heads to the West. They didn't bow because they liked Jesus Christ or because they liked white folks. Machiavelli said a long time ago that "people obey masters for one of two reasons. Either they love them, or they fear them." I often ask myself whether the West believes the Third World obeys them out of love.

It's clear that they feared them; the West with its guns and its power and its might came into Africa, Asia, Latin America, and the U.S.A., and raped them. And while they raped they used beautiful terms: they told the Indians, "We're civilizing you, and we're taming the West. And if you won't be civilized, we'll kill you." So they committed genocide and stole the land, and put the Indians on reservations, and they said that they had civilized the country.

They weren't satisfied with that. They came to Africa and stole Africans and brought them to the U.S.A., and we were being brought there because we were cannibals and we ate each other, and they were going to give us a better life, which was, of course, slavery.

Now I want to make just one clear distinction, before I move on, about cultural integrity. Inside the countries of the West there was democracy for the whites, at least some form of it. But that democracy was at the expense of non-white people. While Britain surely enjoyed her Parliament House nonsense about constitutionality, she was suppressing all of Africa. The same holds true for France, and the same thing, of course, is true today for the United States.

White people are very funny, you know. De Gaulle got out of Vietnam a few years ago, and now he's got very broad-minded. But he's still in Somaliland.

The West said, "Our culture is better, we are civilized." And because of whites' power, the non-white countries began to try to imitate Europe and to imitate its ways, and then some began to believe the whites, because nobody wanted to be uncivilized. Our ancestors knew what civilization was, long before Europeans even got out of their caves, and if they had stuck to their way of life, perhaps we wouldn't be in the shape we are in today.

Thus all other people have been stripped of their culture. They have been forced to accept a culture that does not belong to them. The minds of people of color around the world are so messed up that in certain sections of Vietnam today, and in Japan certainly, women who have slanted eyes are cutting their skin so they can have round eyes and look like Westerners. There's no need to say what black people have been doing to their hair, especially females: they have been putting hot combs in their hair, straightening it, attempting to look like white people, because the West has defined beauty as that which was theirs.

Now there's a fight for cultural integrity in the world today. Each group of people wants to retain its own integrity, and say, "To hell with the West and its culture. Let it keep it. We want ours." I don't propose to speak for the Red Guards, but I would assume that's part of the fight they're waging. It's a healthy fight and it needs to be waged. I know that in the United States one of the fights we're waging is the fight for cultural integrity.

We want to be able to recognize the contributions that the non-white peoples of the world have made. It's amazing: when you do some reading, you find out that they did most of what the white people claim *they* did. They just bleached history. Pythagoras didn't give you geometry, the Egyptians did.

I have something against England, I really do, because when I was young I had to read all that rot about how good England was to Trinidad, while she was raping us left and right. And all I used to read about when I was small was London, the beauty of London, and how peacefully everybody lived, and how nice life was—at my expense. And I used to say, "I sure would like to get to London and burn it down to the ground." But that's violence!

I'm amazed when I pick up the paper and read that "England today decided to give independence to the West Indies." The whole West feels it has the right to *give* everybody their independence. That's totally absurd. You can never *give* anyone his independence. All men are born free, they are enslaved by other men; so the only act that the men who enslaved them can do is, not give them their independence, but stop oppressing them. There's a very important difference, and I don't think people make that all the time. Who the hell is England to give me my independence? All they can do is stop oppressing me, get off my back. But when they say "We're giving you your independence: You're ready for it now," it sounds so much nicer than for them to admit to themselves, "We're going to stop oppressing you because we're becoming a little bit more civilized, or because you're making it uncomfortable for us and we can no longer afford to oppress you at the price that you're asking us to pay." That would be correct. But you wouldn't expect self-condemnation.

You cannot grant anybody independence, they just take it; and that is what white America is going to learn. No white liberal can give me anything. The only thing a white liberal can do for me is to help civilize other whites, because they need to be civilized.

Now in the United States—and England isn't far behind —it is estimated that in another five to ten years, two-thirds of the twenty million black people who inhabit the United States will be living in the ghettos in the heart of the cities. Joining us are going to be hundreds of thousands of Puerto Ricans, Mexican-Americans, and American Indians. The American city, in essence, is going to be populated by the peoples of the Third World, while the white middle classes will flee to the suburbs. Now the black people do not control, nor do we own, the resources— we do not control the land, the houses or the stores. These are all owned by whites who live outside the community. These are very real colonies, in the sense that they are capital and cheap labor exploited by those who live outside the cities. It is white power that makes the laws, and enforces those laws with guns and nightsticks in the hands of white racist policemen and their black mercenaries. It does not seem that the men who control the power and resources of the United States ever sat down and designed those black enclaves, and formally articulated the terms of their colonial and dependent status, as was done, for example, by the apartheid government of South Africa, which Britain, the United States, and France back. Yet one cannot distinguish between one ghetto and another as one moves around the United States; every ghetto seems to be the same. Note that the United States has, on its continental borders, forty-eight states, and each of these states has a ghetto in each of its major cities. As one moves from city to city, it is as though some malignant, racist planning unit had designed each ghetto from one master blueprint. Indeed, if the ghettos had been formally and deliberately planned instead of growing spontaneously and inevitably from the racist functionings of the various institutions that combine to make the society, it would be somehow less frightening—one could understand their similarity as being artificially and consciously imposed, rather than the result of identical patterns of white racism which repeat themselves in cities as far apart as Boston is from Watts— that is 3,000 miles.

A capitalist system automatically includes racism, whether by design or not. Capitalism and racism go hand in hand. The struggle for Black Power in the United States, and certainly around the world, is the struggle to free these colonies from external domination, but we do not seek merely to create communities where black rulers replace white rulers, controlling the lives of black masses, and where black money goes into a few black pockets. We want to see it go into the communal pocket—the society we seek to build among black people is not an oppressive capitalist society. Capitalism, by its very nature, cannot create structures free from exploitation.

The struggle to free these internal colonies relates to the struggles of imperialism around the world. We realistically survey our numbers, and know that it is not possible for black people to take over the whole of the United States militarily, and hold large areas of land; in a highly industrialized nation, the struggle is different. The heart of production, and the heart of commercial trade, is in the cities. We are in the cities. We can become, and are becoming, a disruptive force in the flow of services, goods, and capital. While we disrupt internally and aim for the eye of the octopus, we are hoping that our brothers are disrupting externally to sever the tentacles of the United States. Newark, New Jersey, is where Engelhart has his capital—and for the last five days he couldn't do any work. You know Engelhart controls most of South Africa, along with Rockefeller, the liberal.

It is sometimes said that the African-American movement in the United States does not understand the true nature of the struggle in the world today, that the movement is involved in fighting only racial discrimination, and only with the weapon of nonviolence. It used to be. We moved away from that. The integration movement's goals were middle-class—such as job opportunities for college graduates, open public accommodations. And that's very important because the West doesn't understand its own racism when they talk about integration. White Americans' concept of integration is based on the assumption that there was nothing of value in the black community and that little of value would ever come from the black community. When they talk about integration, they talk about accepting black people—isn't that ridiculous? I have to talk about whether or not I want to accept them, and they're never willing to talk about that, because they know they'll come up losing. Integration is absolutely absurd unless you can talk about it on a two-way street, where black people sit down and decide about integration.

As you know, the Black Power movement that SNCC initiated moved away from the integration movement. Because of the integration movement's middle-class orientation, because of its subconscious racism, and because of its nonviolent approach, it has never been able to involve the black proletariat. It could never attract and hold the young bloods who clearly understood the savagery of white America, and who were ready to meet it with armed resistance. It is the young bloods especially who contain the hatred Che Guevera speaks of:

> Hatred as an element of the struggle, relentless hatred of the enemy that impels us over and beyond the natural limitations of man, and transforms us into effective, violent, selected and cold killing machines.

The Black Power movement has been the catalyst for the bringing together of these young bloods. This is the real revolutionary proletariat, ready to fight by any means necessary, for the liberation of our people.

The Black Power movement in the United States is exposing the extent of the racism and exploitation that permeate all the institutions in the country. It has unique appeal to young black students on campuses across America. These students have been deluded by the fiction that if the black man would educate himself and behave himself, he would be acceptable enough to leave the ranks of the oppressed and have tea with the Queen. However, this year, when provoked by savage white policemen, students on many campuses fought back—before, they had accepted these incidents without rebellion. As students are a part of these rebellions, they begin to acquire a resistance-consciousness. They begin to realize that white America might let a very few of them escape, one by one, into the mainstream of a society, but as soon as blacks move in concert around their blackness she will reply with the fury that reveals her true racist nature.

It is necessary to understand that our analysis of this country and international capitalism begins in race. Color and culture were, and are, key in our oppression; therefore our analysis of history and our economic analysis are rooted in these concepts. Our historical analysis, for example, views the United States as being conceived in racism. Although the first settlers themselves were escaping from oppression, and although their armed uprising against their mother country was around the aggravation of colonialism, and their slogan was, "No taxation without representation," the white European settlers could not extend their lofty theories of democracy to the red men, whom they exterminated systematically as they expanded into the red men's land. Indeed, in the same town where the settlers set up their model of government based on the theory of representative democracy, that same town brought the first slaves in from Africa. The glorious

Constitution's guarantees of "Life, liberty, the pursuit of happiness," and all that other garbage, were guarantees for white men only; the black man was counted only as three-fifths of a person. If you read the United States Constitution, you will see this clause is still in there, to this very day—a black man is three-fifths of a man.

It was because white America needed cheap or free labor that she raped our African homeland of millions of black people. Because we were black and considered inferior, our enslavement was justified and rationalized by the so-called white Christians. They explained their crimes with lies about civilizing the heathens, the savages from Africa, whom they portrayed as being "better off" in the Americas than they'd been in their homeland. These circumstances laid the base and framework for the racism that has become institutionalized in white American society.

In our economic analysis, our interpretation of Marx comes not only from his writing, but, as we see it, from the relationship of capitalistic countries to people of color around the world. The labor movement gives an example of what happens when people in a white country in the West organize themselves when they're being oppressed. The labor movement in the United States is cited around the world as the real friend of the black man, which is going to be able to help him. When the white workers organize—and this is true for all the little white countries—here's how they get out of the bind.

In the beginning, certainly some of the great labor-movement leaders struggled against the industrial lords' absolute control of the economy, but the fight of white workers in the West has been essentially only for money. Those few who had visions of extending the fight, of demanding workers' control of production, never succeeded in transmitting their entire vision to the rank and file. The labor movement found itself asking the industrial lords not to give up their control, but merely to pass out a few more of the fruits of this control. Thus did the United States anticipate the prophecy of Marx, and avoided the inevitable class struggle within the country by expanding into the Third World and exploiting the resources and slave labor of people of color. Britain and France did the same thing. United States capitalists never cut down on their domestic profits to share with the workers—instead, they expanded internationally, and threw the crumbs from their profits to the American working class, who lapped them up. The American working class enjoys the fruits of the labors of the Third World workers. The proletariat has become the Third World, and the bourgeoisie is white Western society.

I've watched the relationships of whites to whites who are communist, and whites to non-whites whom they call communist. When the United States wants to take somebody's country, they get up and say: "Communists are invading them and terrorist guerrilla warfare is on the way, and we must protect democracy, so send thousands of troops to Vietnam to kill the communists." Italy is a white country. Over one-third of its population is communist. Why doesn't the United States invade Italy? Tito is an acknowledged communist. The United States gives him aid. Why don't they invade Tito's country, if they really care about stopping communism? The United States is not kidding anybody; when they want to take over some non-whites' land, they talk about communist aggression—that's what they did in Cuba, in Santo Domingo, and it's what they're doing in Vietnam. They're always telling non-white people how they're going to stop them from going communist. Don't talk about dictatorship. Franco is perhaps the worst dictator in the world today, but the United States gives him aid.

It is clearly not a question of communist invasion, merely a question of taking the countries they want most, and the countries they want most are the non-white countries because that is where the resources of the world are today. That's where they have been for the last few centuries. And that's why white Western society has to be there.

Another mystification white society uses is the word "riot"—when rebellions break out in the large cities of America, the first thing people say is that they're riots. And white Western society is very good, the next thing they say is: "We must have law and order." Hitler had the most efficient system of law and order we've ever seen. He happened to have been a fascist. He did not have justice coupled with his law and order. The United States knows about law and order, it doesn't know about justice. It is for white Western society to talk about law and order. It is for the Third World to talk about justice.

For God's sake, I don't understand how the white West can ever talk about violence—they are the most violent people on the face of the earth. They have used violence to get everything they have. And yet, they're the first to talk about violence. The armed rebellions and the guerrilla warfare going on in the United States today are not the most violent things going on in the world—Vietnam, South Africa, Zimbabwe, Hong Kong, Aden, Somaliland, that's where your violence really is. Violence can take the form of physical warfare, or it can take the form of a slow death. The Jews in the Warsaw ghettos were suffering from violence. It didn't take an actual physical form until they were put in the gas chambers, but they were suffering from mental violence. Wherever you go in Africa today, the Africans are suffering from violence inflicted on them by the white West, be it that they are stripped of their culture, of their human dignity, or of the resources of their very land.

And it is crystal clear to the peoples of the Third World today that it's time out for talk. There can be no talk about how to stop violence, that's clear. Even Camus talks about that, though he cops out. Camus talks about executioner/victim. He says, Well, there are executioner/ victim relationships in society, and the executioner uses force to keep his victim down. But the victim gets tired of that, and what happens is that when the victim moves either to a position of equality or to try to conquer the executioner, he uses the force and the means and the methods that his oppressor used to keep him down. That happens to be violence. I never get caught up with violence. As a matter of fact, one of my favorite quotes that stops all the talk about it is from Sartre:

> What then did you expect when you unbound the gag that had muted those black mouths? That they would chant your praises? Did you think that when those heads that our fathers had forcefully bowed down to the ground were raised again, you would find adoration in their eyes?

That's Jean-Paul Sartre, not me.

We are working to increase the revolutionary consciousness of black people in America to join with the Third World. Whether or not violence is used is not decided by us, but by the white West. We are fighting a political warfare. Politics is war without violence. War is politics with violence. The white West will make the decision on how they want the political war to be fought. We are not any longer going to bow our heads to any white man. If he touches one black man in the United States, he is going to go to war with every black man in the United States.

We are going to extend our fight internationally and we are going to hook up with the Third World. It is the only salvation—we are fighting to save our humanity. We are indeed fighting to save the humanity of the world, which the West has failed miserably to preserve. And the fight must be waged from the Third World. There will be new speakers. They will be Che, they will be Mao, they will be Fanon. You can have Rousseau, you can have Marx, you can even have the great libertarian John Stuart Mill.

I want to tell you why violence is important in building a resistance-consciousness in the United States. I want to use a quote that we learned from Germany:

> The triumph of the Storm Troopers required that the tortured victim allow himself to be led to the gallows without protesting, that he repudiate and abandon himself to the point where he ceased to affirm his identity.

There is nothing more terrible than these processions of human beings going to their death like zombies. I'm afraid that blacks in America cannot afford to march to the gallows the way Jews did. If white America decides to play Nazi, we're going to let them know the black people are not Jews, we're going to fight back to the death. And lest you think that sounds very violent, let me remind you of a poem that your "great" Prime Minister Sir Winston Churchill read when you were getting ready to attack Germany, even though you were told that you were a minority. Incidentally, I don't know if he told you, it was written by a black man named Claude McKay from Jamaica, and he wrote it for black people. It is called "If We Must Die." It is our poem today in the United States:

If we must die, let it not be like hogs
Hunted and penned in an inglorious spot,
While round us bark the mad and hungry dogs,
Making their mock at our accursed lot.
If we must die, O let us nobly die,
So that our precious blood may not be shed
In vain; then even the monsters we defy
Shall be constrained to honor us though dead!

94

O kinsmen! we must meet the common foe!
Though far outnumbered let us show us brave,
And for their thousand blows deal one deathblow!
What though before us lies the open grave?
Like men we'll face the murderous, cowardly pack,
Pressed to the wall, dying, but fighting back!

Our fight will be international because such a consciousness will destroy the minority complex within black communities that is so carefully calculated by the American press; and also because when the black man realizes that the counter-insurgency efforts of the United States are directed against his brothers, he will not fight in any of its wars—he will not go. Then it will become crystal clear to the world that the imperialist wars of the U.S. are nothing less than racist wars. During the past year we have initiated a black resistance movement to the draft, which is being led by our hero, the World Champion, Mr. Muhammad Ali. We're against black men fighting their brothers in Vietnam—and we're certain that the next Vietnam will either be in the Congo, South Africa, Zimbabwe, Bolivia, Guatemala, Brazil, Peru, or indeed in the West Indies. And we are not going to fight our brothers.

For the past four hundred years the African-American has tried to coexist peacefully inside the United States. It has been to no avail. We have never lynched a white man, we have never burned their churches, we have never bombed their houses, we have never beaten them in the streets. I wish we could say the same for white people around the world. Our history demonstrates that the reward for trying to coexist in peace has been the physical and psychological murder of our peoples. We have been lynched, our houses have been bombed and our churches burned. Now we are being shot down like dogs in the streets by white racist policemen. We can no longer accept this oppression without retribution. We understand that as we expand our resistance and internationalize the consciousness of our people, as our martyred brother Malcolm X did, we will get retaliation from the government, as he did. As the resistance struggle escalates we are well aware of Che's words: "The struggle will not be a mere street fight, but it will be a long and harsh struggle." And to the end, we are going to work with our common brothers and sisters in the Third World to fight this oppression.

I would like to conclude by telling you just precisely what black people in America are going to do, and when we're going to do it, and how we're going to do it, and why we're going to do it. This is your only chance to hear it clear, because you'll be hearing it from the BBC next time.

Black people in the United States have no time to play nice polite parlor games, especially when the lives of our children are at stake. Some white Americans can afford to speak softly, tread lightly, employ the soft-sell and the put-off—or is it put-down?—because they own the society. For us to adopt their methods of relieving our oppression is certainly ludicrous. We blacks must respond in our own way, on our own terms, in a manner that fits our temperaments. The definition of ourselves, the road we pursue, and the goals we seek, are our responsibility. It is clear that society is capable of, and willing to, reward those individuals who do not forcefully condemn it—to reward them with prestige, status, and material benefits—but these crumbs of corruption will be rejected. As a people we have absolutely nothing to lose by refusing to play such games. Anything less than clarity, honesty, and forcefulness perpetuates the centuries of sliding over, dressing up and soothing down the true feelings, hopes, and demands of an oppressed black people. Mild demands and hypocritical smiles mislead white America into thinking that all is fine and peaceful; they lead white America into thinking that the path and pace whites choose for dealing with racial problems are acceptable to the masses of blacks. It is far better to speak forcefully and truthfully. Only when one's true self, black or white, is exposed, can society proceed to deal with the problems from a position of clarity, and not from one of misunderstanding.

Thus, we have no intention of engaging in the meaningless language so common to discussions of race in the world today: "Things were and are bad, but we are making progress." "Granted, your demands are legitimate, but we cannot move hastily. Stable societies are best built slowly." "Be careful that you do not anger or alienate your white allies. Remember, after all, you are only 10 per cent of the population."

We reject the language and the views, whether expressed by blacks or by whites. We leave them to others to mouth, because we don't feel that this rhetoric is either relevant or useful. Rather we suggest a more meaningful language —that of Frederick Douglass, a man who understood the nature of protest in society:

> Those who profess to favor freedom, yet deprecate agitation, are men who want crops without ploughing up the ground. . . . Power concedes nothing without demands—it never did and it never will. . . . The limits of tyrants are prescribed by the endurance of those whom they oppress.

He was a slave.

Black Power, to us, means that black people see themselves as a part of a new force, sometimes called the Third World; that we see our struggle as closely related to liberation struggles around the world. We must hook up with these struggles. We must, for example, ask ourselves: when black people in Africa begin to storm Johannesburg, what will be the reaction of the United States? It seems inevitable that the U.S. will move to protect its

financial interests in South Africa, which means protecting the white rule in South Africa, as England has
already done. What will be the role of black people living
inside the United States? Black people in the United
States have the responsibility to oppose, and if not to
oppose, certainly to neutralize white America's efforts.
This is but one example. Many such situations have already arisen around the world, and there are more to
come, there is only one place for blacks in America in
these struggles, and that is on the side of the Third World.
Frantz Fanon, in *The Wretched of the Earth*, puts forth
clearly the reasons for the relationship of the concept
called Black Power to the concept of a new force in the
world:

> Let us decide not to imitate Europe. . . . Let us
> try to create the whole man, whom Europe has
> been incapable of bringing to triumphant birth.
> Two centuries ago a former European colony de-
> cided to catch up with Europe. It succeeded so
> well that the U.S.A. became a monster in which
> the taints, the sickness and the inhumanity of Eu-
> rope has grown to appalling dimensions. . . . The
> Third World today faces Europe like a colossal
> mass, whose aim should be to try to resolve the
> problems to which Europe has not been able to find
> the answers. . . . It is a question of the Third
> World starting a new history of man, a history
> which will have regard to the sometimes prodi-
> gious thesis which Europe has put forward, but
> which will also not forget Europe's crimes, of
> which the most horrible was committed in the
> heart of man and consisted of the pathological
> tearing apart of his functions and the crumbling
> away of his unity. . . .
> No, there is no question of a return to nature.
> It is simply a very concrete question of not drag-

ging men towards mutilation, of not imposing upon them brain rhythms which very quickly obliterate it and wreck it. The pretext of catching up must not be used for pushing men around, to tear him away from himself or from his privacy, to break and to kill him.

No, we do not want to catch up with anyone. What we want to do is go forward all the time, night and day, in the company of man, in the company of all men. . . .

Since there's been a lot of talk about psychology at this meeting, I've thought up a psychological problem. White liberals are always saying, "What can we do?" I mean, they're always coming to help black people. I thought of an analogy. If you were walking down the street and a man had a gun on another man—let's say both of them were white—and you had to help somebody, whom would you help? It's obvious to me that if I were walking down the street, and a man had a gun on another man, and I was going to help, I'd help the man who didn't have the gun, if the man who had the gun was just pulling the gun on the other man for no apparent reason—if he was just going to rob him or shoot him because he didn't like him. The only way I could help is either to get a gun and shoot the man with the gun, or take the gun away from him— join the fellow who doesn't have a gun and both of us gang up on the man with the gun. But white liberals never do that. When the man has the gun, they walk around him and they come to the victim, and they say "Let me help you," and what they mean is "help you adjust to the situation with the man who has the gun on you."

If indeed white liberals are going to help, their only job is to get the gun from the man and talk to him, because he is a sick man. The black man is not the sick man, it is the white man who is sick, he's the one who picked up the gun first.

So you can see that psychologists ought to stop investigating and examining people of color, they ought to investigate and examine their own corrupt society. That's where they belong. And once they are able to do that, then maybe we can move on to build in the Third World.

I want to read a poem that was written by a young man who works in SNCC, the organization for which I work. His name is Worth Long. It's called "Arson and Cold Grace, or How I Yearn to Burn, Baby Burn":

We have found you out, false-faced Americans, we have
found you out.
We have found you out, false-faced farmers, we have
found you out.
The sparks of suspicion are melting your waters
And waters can't drown them, the fires are burning
And firemen can't calm them with falsely appeasing
And preachers can't pray with hopes for deceiving
Nor leaders deliver a lecture on losing
Nor teachers inform whom the chosen are choosing
For now is the fire and fires won't answer
To logical reason and hopefully seeming
Hot flames must devour the kneeling and feeling

And torture the masters whose idiot pleading
Gets lost in the echoes of dancing and bleeding.
We have found you out, false-faced farmers, we have
found you out.
We have found you out, false-faced America, we have
found you out.

8

Solidarity
with
Latin
America

We share with you a common struggle, it becomes increasingly clear; we have a common enemy. Our enemy is white Western imperialist society. Our struggle is to overthrow this system that feeds itself and expands itself through the economic and cultural exploitation of nonwhite, non-Western peoples—of the Third World.

We share with you also a common vision of the establishment of humanistic societies in the place of those now existing. We seek, with you, to change the power bases of

First Conference of the Organization of Latin American Solidarity, Cuba, July, 1967—after London.

the world—mankind will share the resources of their nations instead of having to give them up to foreign plunderers; civilizations will be able to retain their cultural sovereignty instead of being forced to submit to foreign rulers, who impose their own corrupt cultures on those civilizations they would dominate.

Anglo* society has been nearly successful in keeping all of us, the oppressed of the Third World, separated and fragmented. They do this for their survival; if we felt our unity we would know our strength. For hundreds of years here on this continent, where the Anglo is in the minority, he has succeeded in keeping all of us who are oppressed from realizing our common plight. But the call of Che Guevara for a continental struggle against a common enemy would seem to ameliorate this fragmentation among those who would resist Western imperialism. We speak with you, comrades, because we wish to make clear that we understand that our destinies are intertwined. Our world can only be the Third World; our only struggle, for the Third World; our only vision, of the Third World.

Until recently, most African-Americans thought that the best way to alleviate their oppression was through attempts at integration into the society. If we could enjoy public accommodations in the United States—motels, hotels, restaurants, and so forth—our condition would be bettered, many of us believed.

This attitude was characteristic of the "civil rights movement" and clearly points up the bourgeois character of that "movement." Only the bourgeoisie are in a position to be concerned about public accommodations. The African-American masses, on the other hand, do not have any jobs, any housing worthy of the name "decent," nor the money to enjoy restaurants, hotels, and motels. The

* "Anglo" is a term used by Latin Americans and Spanish-speaking persons in the United States to denote Anglo-Saxons and other non-Spanish-speaking Europeans.

civil rights movement did not actively involve the masses, because it did not speak to the needs of the masses.

Nonetheless, the civil rights movement was a beginning, and because its aims met resistance throughout the United States, depths of racism heretofore unrecognized were laid bare. It had been thought that the aims of the civil rights movement would be easily realizable, because the United States Constitution supported them. But thousands of African-Americans were jailed, intimidated, and beaten, and some were murdered, for agitating for those rights that are guaranteed by the Constitution but are only available to whites.

Eventually, Congress passed a civil rights bill and a voting rights bill, assuring us of those rights for which we had been agitating. By this time, however, more and more of us were realizing that our problems would not be solved by the enacting of these laws. In fact, these laws did not begin to speak to our problems. Our problems were an inherent part of the capitalist system and therefore could not be alleviated within that system.

The African-American masses had been outside the civil rights movement. For four years they watched to see if any significant changes would come from the nonviolent demonstrations—it became clear that nothing would change. In the summer of 1964, only a couple of weeks after the civil rights bill was passed, the first of what are now more than one hundred rebellions occurred. The following year, the same year that the voting rights bill was enacted, one of the largest rebellions occurred in Watts. These rebellions were violent uprisings in which African-Americans exchanged gunfire with police and army troops, burned down stores, and took from the stores those commodities that are rightfully ours—food and clothing that we had never had. These rebellions are increasing in intensity and frequency each year; now practically every major city has seen us rise to say, We will seize the day or be killed in the attempt.

We are moving to control our African-American communities as you are moving to wrest control of your countries, of the entire Latin continent, from the hands of foreign imperialist powers. There is only one course open to us: we must change North America so that the economy and politics of the country will be in the hands of the people, and our particular concern is our people, African-Americans. But it is clear that a community based on the community ownership of all resources could not exist within the present capitalist framework. For the total transformation to take place, whites must see the struggle that we're engaged in as being their own struggle. At the present time, they do not. Even though the white worker is exploited, he sees his own best interest lying with the power structure. Because of the racist nature of this country, we cannot work in white communities, but we have asked those whites who work with us to go into their own communities to begin propagandizing and organizing. When the white workers realize their true condition, then alliances will be possible between ourselves and them.

But we cannot wait for this to happen, or despair if it does not happen. The struggle we are engaged in is international. We know very well that what happens in Vietnam affects our struggle here and what we do affects the struggle of the Vietnamese people. This is even more apparent when we look at ourselves not as African-Americans of the United States, but as African-Americans of the Americas. At the present moment, the power structure has sown the seeds of hate and discord between African-Americans and Spanish-speaking people in the large cities where they live. In the state of California, African-Americans and Spanish-speaking people together comprise almost 50 per cent of the population, yet the two view each other with suspicion and, sometimes, outright hostility. We recognize this as the old trick of "divide and conquer" and we are working to see that it does not succeed this time. Last week Puerto Ricans and blacks took the streets together in New York City to fight against the police—which demonstrates success in this area. Our destiny cannot be separated from the destiny of the Spanish-speaking people in the United States and of the Americas. Our victory will not be achieved unless they celebrate their liberation side by side with us, for it is not their struggle, but our struggle together. We have already pledged ourselves to do what we are asked to do to aid the struggle for the independence of Puerto Rico, to free it from domination by U.S. business and military interests; and we look upon Cuba as a shining example of hope in our hemisphere. We do not view our struggle as being contained within the boundaries of the United States as they are defined by present-day maps—instead, we look to the day when a true United States of America will extend from Tierra del Fuego to Alaska, when those formerly oppressed will stand together, a liberated people.

Our people are a colony within the United States, and you are colonies outside the United States. It is more than a figure of speech to say that the black communities in America are the victims of white imperialism and colonial exploitation—in practical economic and political terms it is true. There are over thirty million of us in the United States. For the most part we live in sharply defined sections of the rural black-belt areas and the shanty towns of the South, and more and more in the slums of the Northern and Western industrial cities. With us there are hundreds and thousands of Puerto Ricans, Mexican-Americans and American Indians. American cities are in essence populated by people of the Third World, while the white middle-class flees. The heart of commercial trade is in these cities—but though we live there, we do not control our resources. We do not control the land, the houses, or the stores. They are owned by whites who live outside the community.

Since 1966 the cry of the rebellions has been Black

Power. This cry implies an ideology that the masses understand instinctively. It is because we are powerless that we are oppressed—and it is only with power that we can make the decisions governing our lives and our communities. Those who have power have everything; those who are without power have nothing. Without power we have to beg for what is rightfully ours. With power we will take our birthright because it was with power that our birthright was taken from us.

Black Power is more than a slogan; it is a way of looking at our problems and the beginning of a solution to them. It attacks racism and exploitation, the horns of the bull that seek to gore us.

The United States is a racist country. From its very beginning it has built itself upon the subjugation of colored people. To enslave another human being, one needs a justification, and the United States has always found this justification in proclaiming the superiority of whites and the inferiority of non-whites. We are called "niggers"; Spanish-speaking people are called "spics"; the Chinese, "chinks"; the Vietnamese, "gooks." Dehumanizing people of color makes it just, in the mind of the white man, that we should be enslaved, exploited, and oppressed.

When a man himself can be convinced that he is inferior, it becomes even easier to keep that man a slave. How much easier to put a man in chains by making him believe he is inferior! As long as he does, he will keep himself in chains. As long as a slave allows himself to be defined as a slave by the master, he will be a slave, even if the master dies. This technique has been successfully practiced not only against us, but wherever people have been enslaved, oppressed and exploited. We can see it happening today in the schools of large American cities, where Puerto Rican and Mexican children are not allowed to speak Spanish and are taught nothing of their country and their history. It is apparent in many African countries, where one is not considered educated unless he has studied in France and speaks French.

Black power attacks this brainwashing by saying, *We will define ourselves.* We will no longer accept the white man's definition of ourselves as ugly, ignorant, and uncultured. We will recognize our own beauty and our own culture, and we will no longer be ashamed of ourselves, for a people ashamed of themselves cannot be free.

Because our color has been used as a weapon to oppress us, we must use our color as a weapon of liberation, just as other people use their nationality as a weapon for their liberation. Black Power recognized that we are made to feel inferior so that we may be more easily exploited. But even if we destroyed racism, we would not necessarily destroy exploitation; and if we destroyed exploitation, we would not necessarily end racism. They must both be destroyed; we must constantly launch a two-pronged attack; we must constantly keep our eyes on both of the bull's horns.

The true potential revolutionaries in this country are the people of color in the ghettos, those who have developed insurgence in the African-American and Latin communities, where past rebellions have taught important lessons in dealing with the governments' armed reaction to our uprisings. In the past three years, there have been over one hundred uprisings in the internal colonies of the United States. No doubt these are reported to you as "minor disturbances initiated by a few malcontents"— but these are major rebellions with numbers of participants who are developing a consciousness of resistance. These rebellions should not be taken lightly.

It is with increasing concern that we see the United States will by any means necessary attempt to prevent the liberation struggles sweeping across the Third World, but in particular we know that the United States fears most the liberation struggle on this continent. In order to secure itself geographically, the United States must have

Latin America, economically, politically, and culturally—
it would not do for the Anglos to be isolated in a continent
of hostiles.

Black Power not only addresses itself to exploitation,
but to the problem of cultural integrity. Western society
has always understood the importance of language to a
people's cultural consciousness and integrity. Wherever
imperialism has gone, she has imposed her culture by
force on other peoples, forcing them to adopt her language and way of life. When African slaves were brought
to this country, the Anglo saw that if he took away the
language of the African, he broke one of the bonds that
kept blacks united and struggling. Africans were for-
bidden to speak to each other in their own language; if
they were found doing so, they were savagely beaten. In
Puerto Rico, where Yankee cultural imposition is at its
height, English is taught in all high schools for three
years, and Spanish is taught for two years.

Anglo society learned other valuable lessons from the
enslavement of Africans in this country. If you separate a
man's family, as was done to the slaves, you again weaken
his resistance. But carry the separation further. Take a
few of the weaker slaves and treat them as house pets—the
lighter-skinned slave, the offspring of the master's rape of
the African woman, was preferred. Give him the crumbs
from the master's table and cast-off clothing and soon he
will fear to lose these small comforts. Then use his fears,
get him to report on the activities of the bad slaves, report
the impending revolts and uprisings. Create distrust and
dissent among the Africans, and they will fight among
themelves instead of uniting to fight their oppressors.

Today's descendants of the African slaves brought to
America have been separated from their cultural and
national roots. Black children are not taught the glory of
African civilization in the history of mankind; they are
instead taught that Africa is "the dark continent," in-
habited by man-eating savages. They are not taught about

the thousands of black martyrs who died resisting the white slave masters. They are not taught about the numerous uprisings and revolts, when hundreds of brave Africans refused to submit to slavery. Instead, their history books have "happy slaves singing in their fields . . . content with their new lives." Those "few" slaves who did resist are called "troublemakers," "malcontents," or "crazy."

Black children in North America grow up aspiring only to enter white society—not only because white society eats better, is housed and clothed better, and can make a better living, but also because they have been bombarded by the white-controlled communications media and educated by black teachers with white minds that white is better, white is beautiful. You need Anglo features, manner of speech, and aspirations, if you are to be successful, even *within* the black community. The white man hardly needs to police his colonies within this country, for he has plundered the cultures and enslaved the minds of the people of color until their resistance is paralyzed by self-hate.

An important fight in the Third World therefore is the fight for cultural integrity. Wherever Western society has gone, as Frantz Fanon tells us, she has imposed her culture through force. The people of a conquered country begin to believe that Western culture is better than their own. The young people begin to put aside the richness of their native culture to take on the tinsel of Western culture. They become ashamed of their roots, and inevitably they are trapped in a life of self-hate and private pursuit for self-gain. Thus does the West entrap whole peoples with little resistance. One of our major battles is to root out corrupt Western values, and our resistance cannot prevail unless our cultural integrity is restored and maintained.

It is from our people's history, therefore, that we know our struggles and your struggles are the same. We have difficulty getting the information we need on what is happening in your countries. In so many ways we are illiterate—we don't know of your heroes, your battles, and your victories. But we are working now to increase the consciousness of the African-American so it will extend internationally—and the United States fears this more than anything else.

9

We're here to celebrate Brother Huey P. Newton's birthday. We're not here to celebrate it as Huey Newton the individual, but as Huey Newton part and parcel of black people wherever we are in the world today. In talking about Brother Huey Newton tonight, we have to talk about the struggle of black people—not only in the United States but in the world today and how we become part and parcel of the struggle, how we move on so that our people will survive America.

Speech given at the birthday benefit party for Brother Huey P. Newton, Minister of Defense of the Black Panther Party for Self-Defense, Oakland Auditorium, Oakland, Calif., February 17, 1968.

We are not talking about politics tonight, we're not talking about economics tonight, we are talking about the survival of a race of people. That is all that is at stake.

Why is it necessary for us to talk about the survival of our people? Many of us feel—many of our generation feel—that the white folks are getting ready to commit genocide against us. Now, many people think that's a horrible thing to say, but as Brother Malcolm said, we should examine history.

The birth of this nation was conceived in the genocide of the red man. In order for this country to come about, the honky had to completely exterminate the red man, and he did it! And now he doesn't even feel sorry; he romanticizes it on television with cowboys and Indians. The question we must ask ourselves is, If he's capable of doing it to the red man, can he also do it to us?

Let us examine history some more. People say it is a horrible thing to say that white people would think about committing genocide against black people. Let us check our history. It is a fact that we built this country, nobody else. When this country started, economically it was an agricultural country. The cash crop on the world market was cotton. We picked the cotton! And we fought in the wars of this country. We built this country.

This country is becoming more and more technological, so that the need for black people is disappearing fast. When the need for black people disappears, so will we. The white man will consciously wipe us out.

Let us check World War II. He will not do it unto his own. Notice who he dropped an atomic bomb on, some helpless yellow people in Hiroshima, some *helpless* yellow people. If you do not think he's *capable* of committing genocide against us, check out what he's doing to our brothers in Vietnam. We have to understand that we're talking about our survival—whether or not this beautiful race of people is going to survive on the earth.

Check out the white race. Wherever they have gone they

112

have ruled, conquered, murdered, and plagued—whether they are the majority or the minority they *always* rule. Check out the pattern in which they move. They came to this country and didn't know a damn thing about it. The red man showed them how to adapt. He showed them how to grow corn. He showed them how to hunt. And when the Indians finished showing them *they wiped them out!*

The white man wasn't satisfied. He went to South America. The Aztec Indians said: "This is our silver, this is our copper, these are our metals, these are our statues. We built them for the beauty of our people." After the Indians showed their wealth to him, he took it and *he wiped them out!*

The white man went to Africa. Our ancestors said: "Dig, this is our way of life. We beat drums, we enjoy ourselves, we have gold, we make diamonds and stuff for our women." He took the gold, he made us slaves, and today he *runs* Africa. He went to Asia. The Chinese showed him everything they had. They showed him gunpowder. They said: "We use this for fireworks on our anniversaries, on our days of festivities." He took it, he made it a gun, and he conquered China.

We are talking about a certain type of superiority complex that exists in the white man wherever he is. That's what we have to understand today. So that everything else goes out the window, we talk about survival. They can cut all the junk about poverty programs, education, housing, welfare. We're talking about survival— and brothers and sisters, we're going to survive America.

We have to understand what is going on not only in this country but in the world, especially in Africa. Because we are an African people, we have *always* maintained our own value system.

Our people have resisted for 413 years in this wilderness. And they resisted so that *this* generation can carry out what must be done. We cannot fail our ancestors.

We resisted in every way you can point to. Take the English language. There are cats who come here from Italy, from Germany, from Poland, from France—in two generations they speak English perfectly. We have *never* spoken English perfectly. And that is because our people consciously resisted a language that did not belong to us. Never did, never will, anyhow they try to run it down our throat, we ain't gonna have it. We ain't gonna have it! You must understand that as a level of resistance. Anybody can speak that simple honky's language correctly. We have not done it because we have resisted.

Check out our way of life. No matter how hard he's tried, we still maintain a communal way of life in our community. We do not send old people to old people's homes—that's junk. We do not call children illegitimate; we take care of any child in our community. It is a level of resistance that we must begin to look for among our people. Pick up that thread and do what has to be done so that our people will survive.

Three things: first and foremost, the honky has been able to make us hate each other. He has channeled our love for each other into love for his country—*his* country. We must begin to develop—and this is the most important thing we can do as a people—*we must develop an undying love for our people, our people.* We must develop the undying love personified by Brother Huey P. Newton. Undying love for our people. If we do not do that, we will be wiped out. Our slogan will become: first, our people; then, and only then, me and you as individuals. Our people first.

Second, comes the slogan: Every Negro is a potential black man. We *will not* alienate him. And we must understand the concept of Negro and the concept of black man. We came to this country as black men and as Africans. It took us four hundred years to become Negroes. Understand that. It means that the concept of a black man is one who recognizes his cultural and historical roots. He recognizes that his African ancestors were the greatest warriors on the face of this earth.

Many of our people's minds have been whitewashed. If a Negro comes up to you and you turn your back on him, he's got to run to the honky. We're gonna take time and patience with our people, because they're *ours*. All of the Uncle Toms are *ours*. We're gonna sit down and we're gonna talk, and when they slap we're gonna bow. We're gonna *try* to bring them home; and if they don't come home, we gonna off them, that's all.

We have to recognize who our major enemy is. The major enemy is not your brother, flesh of your flesh and blood of your blood. The major enemy is the honky and his institutions of racism—*that* is the major enemy. And whenever anybody prepares for revolutionary warfare, you concentrate on the major enemy. We're not strong enough to fight each other and also fight him. We will not fight each other today. There will be no fights in the black community among black people, there will just be people who will be offed! There will be no fights, there will be no disruptions. We are going to be united.

Third, and most important, we must understand that for black people the question of community is not a question of geography, it is a question of color. If you live in Watts, if you live in Harlem, South Side Chicago, Detroit, West Philadelphia, Georgia, Mississippi, Alabama, wherever you go, the first place you go is to your people. Not to the land, but to your *people*. We must break down the concept that black people living inside the United States are black Americans. That's nonsense! We have brothers in Africa and Cuba, we have brothers in Latin America, we have brothers all over the world. And once we begin to understand that the concept "community" is simply one of "our people," it makes no difference where we are—we are with our people and therefore we are home.

Now then, survival. It is necessary to understand the

moves of our enemy. The United States works on what we call the three Ms—the missionaries, the money, and the marines. That's precisely the way it's moved all over the world; it is the way it moves against *us*. They send the missionaries in—we send them out. They send the money in, with the poverty program—the Vietnamese and the Koreans are pulling the money out. The next thing comes the marines. Comes the marines. And if we're talking seriously, we get prepared for the marines. Now, even if some black people do not think that the white man is going to wipe us out completely, there won't be any harm being prepared just in case he decides to do it. So there'll be no harm in preparing ourselves for the marines.

There are a lot of tactics we can learn. The VC are showing us the best way to get it done. And don't be afraid to say, yeah, you want the Vietnamese to defeat America 'cause they wrong from the jump. Don't get up there and play games with them! You ever see them on T.V.—"Well, actually, we were wrong going into Vietnam but we can't get out unless we save face." To save that honky's face, millions of Vietnamese have to die. That's a lot of junk. If you're wrong, say you're wrong and get out. Get out!

We have to then go down the programs that they run through our throats and see how they relate to us. The first one is the vote. They have a new thing now: "Black Power is the vote." The vote in this country is, has been, and always will be irrelevant to the lives of black people. That is a fact. We survived in Mississippi, Alabama, Georgia, Louisiana, Texas, South Carolina, North Carolina, Virginia, and Washington, D.C., without the vote. Two years ago, Julian Bond was elected by black people in Georgia. They took him off the seat, and there was no representation, but black people in Georgia are still surviving today. They took Adam Clayton Powell out of office, they had him out of office for a year and a half— black people in Harlem are still surviving. That should teach you the vote isn't anything but a honky's trick, nothing but a honky's trick.

If we talk about the vote today, we talk about it as one thing—*an organizing tool to bring our people together, nothing else.* It becomes a vehicle for organization, it cannot be anything else. To believe the vote is going to save you is to believe the way Brother Adam Clayton Powell did. He's in Bimini now.

That's what we have to understand. The second thing they ram down our throat is the poverty program. And you have to understand the poverty program. It is designed, number one, to split the black community, and number two, to split the black family. There is no doubt about its splitting the black community. We know all the people who've started fighting over the crumbs (because that's all the poverty program is—crumbs). If we'd leave the crumbs alone and organize, we could take the whole loaf. It belongs to us.

But what happens is that the poverty program sends a couple of hundred thousand dollars into the community and groups start fighting over that money. So, automatically you've got splits in the community. Watts is the best example that we have to date. It was the first one to get the poverty program after the rebellion and today it is the most divided black community in the country.

We have to recognize what the poverty program does. In any race of people the most instinctively revolutionary group are the youth. Because the youth are always willing to fight at the drop of a hat. In anybody's race. And the poverty program is aimed right at our youth—to stop them from fighting. That's all the poverty program is: stop rebellions—not take care of black people—stop the rebellions. How would you feel if you were a father, and your son, who you were supposed to be providing for, comes home with ninety dollars a week and you are still unemployed? What is the poverty program doing to our fathers? If they were concerned about the black community, if they believed the garbage they run down about the black family, they would give the jobs to our fathers, the breadwinners of our families, so we *could* have some respect for them.

But it is precisely because the poverty program is aimed at quelling our youth that they do that, and all the people who administer the poverty program won't even put their children in those programs that are supposed to be so good for us.

Let us move to education. And we must talk very clearly about this concept of education. Frantz Fanon said very clearly: "Education is nothing but the re-establishment and reinforcement of values and institutions of a given society."

All the brother's saying is that whatever this society says is right, when you go to school they are going to tell you it's right and you got to run it down. If you run it on down you get an A. If as your teacher I say to you, "Columbus discovered America in 1492," and you say, "No, Columbus didn't discover America in 1492, there were *Indians* here," I simply tell you that you flunk the course. So education doesn't mean what they say it means. We must begin to use education for our people.

And we must understand our communities. In our communities there are dope addicts, there are pimps, there are prostitutes, there are hustlers, there are teachers, there are maids, there are porters, there are preachers, there are gangsters. If I go to high school I want to learn how to be a good maid, a good porter, a good hustler, a good pimp, a good prostitute, a good preacher, a good teacher.

Education is supposed to prepare you to live in your community. That's what our community is like. If the educational system cannot do that, it must teach us how to change our community. It must do one or the other. The schools we send our children to do neither; they do something absolutely opposite. And when our youth, who are

118

more intelligent than all those honkies on those school boards, drop out of that school because they recognize it's not going to help them, then we turn around and yell at them, dividing our community again. We have to understand that until we control an educational system that will teach us how to change our community, there's no need to send anybody to school. That's just a natural fact.

We have no alternative but to fight, whether we like it or not. On every level in this country black people have *got* to fight, *got* to fight, *got* to fight.

Let us move down and talk about organizing as a concept. We have the masses and the bourgeoisie in our community of black people. The bourgeoisie is very, very minute inside our community. We have to bring them home. We have to bring them home for many reasons. We must bring them home because they have technical skills that must be used for the benefit of their people, not for the benefit of this country that is against their people. We've got to bring them home. The way to bring our people home is by using patience, love, brotherhood, and unity—not force—love, patience, brotherhood and unity. We try and we try and we try. If they become a threat, we off them.

But we must begin to understand bringing them home in the context of forming a united front inside our community—a black united front that engulfs every sector, so that every facet and every person inside our community is working for the benefit of black people. And that is, for each other's survival. A lot of people in the bourgeoisie tell me they don't like Rap Brown when he says, "I'm gonna burn the country down." But every time Rap Brown says that, they get a poverty program.

A lot of people tell me that they don't like the Black Panthers for Self-Defense walking around with guns. But I tell you now, if the honkies in San Francisco off the fighters, who happen to be the Black Panthers for Self-

Defense (there isn't anybody in this community prepared to fight right now), everybody gets offed. Everybody gets offed.

We need each other. We have to have each other for our survival. We need everyone from the revolutionaries to the conservatives—a Black United Front is what we're about, a Black United Front. Now there are some people who may not understand Brother Rap when he talks about forming alliances. He says we have to ally with Mexican-Americans, Puerto Ricans, and the dispossessed people of the earth. He doesn't mention poor whites. We must understand that. I will not deny that poor whites in this country are oppressed. But there are two types of oppression. One is exploitation, the other is colonization. And we have to understand the difference between them. Exploitation is when you exploit somebody of your own race. Colonization is when you exploit somebody of a different race. *We* are colonized, *they* are exploited.

If I am black and I am exploiting you who are also black, we have the same values, the same culture, the same language, the same society, the same institutions, so I do not have to destroy those institutions for you. But if you are of another race, if you have a different culture, different language, different values, I have to destroy all of those to make you bow to me. And that is the difference between poor black and poor white. Poor whites have their culture, have their values, have their institutions; ours have been completely destroyed.

We need alliances with people who are trying to rebuild their culture, trying to rebuild their history, trying to rebuild their dignity, with people who are fighting for their humanity. Poor white people are not fighting for their humanity, they're fighting for more money. There are a lot of poor white people in this country, and you haven't seen any of them rebel yet, have you? Why is it that black people are rebelling? Do you think it's only because of poor jobs? Don't believe that junk the honky is running down. It's not only poor jobs—it's a question of a people fighting for their culture and their nature, fighting for their *humanity*.

We have been so colonized that we are ashamed to say we hate, and that is the best example of a person who's colonized. You sit in your house, a honky walks in your house, beats you up, rapes your wife, beats up your child, and you don't have the humanity to say, "I hate you." You don't have it. That is how dehumanized we are. We are so dehumanized we cannot say, "Yes, we hate you for what you have done to us"—can't say it. And we are afraid to think beyond that point. Who do you think has more hatred pent up in them, white people for black people or black people for white people? Obviously the hatred has been more from white people for black people. What have we done to them for them to build up this hatred? Absolutely nothing! Yet we don't even want to hate them for what they've done to us. If hate should be justified, we have the best justification of all for hating honkies. But we have been so dehumanized, we're like a dog that the master can throw out the house, that the master can spit on, and whenever he calls, the dog comes running back. We are human beings and we have emotions. We're fighting for our humanity, and in regaining our humanity we recognize all the emotions that are in us. If you have love, you've got to have hate. You don't have one-sided emotions, that's a lot of junk. You always have two sides—hot, cold; white, black—everything goes—love, hate. If you don't have hate, you cannot differentiate love.

That brings us to the point about communism and socialism. The ideologies of communism and socialism speak to class structure, to people who oppress people from the top down to the bottom. We are not just facing exploitation. We are facing something much more important, because we are the victims of racism. In their present form neither communism nor socialism speak to the problem of racism. And to black people in this country, racism comes first, far more important than exploitation. No matter how much money you make in the black community, when you go into the white world you are still a nigger. The question of racism must be uppermost in our minds. How do we destroy those institutions that seek to keep us dehumanized? That is all we're talking about.

Now, for white people who are exploited, the question of communism comes first, because they're exploited by their own people. If you were exploited by other black people, it would be a question of how we divide the profits. It is not that for us. It is a question of how we regain our humanity and begin to live as a people. We do not do that because of the effects of racism in this country. We must therefore consciously strive for an ideology which deals with racism first, and if we do that we recognize the necessity of hooking up with the 900 million black people in the world today.

If we recognize that, then our political situation must become international, it cannot be national. Honkies don't exploit us alone, they exploit the whole Third World—Asia, Africa, Latin America. They take advantage of Europe, but they don't colonize Europe, they colonize Asia, Africa, and Latin America. If we begin to understand that, then the problems America is heading for become uppermost in our minds.

The first one is the conflict in the Middle East. We must declare on whose side we stand. We can be for no one but the Arabs. There can be *no* doubt in our minds at all. We can be for no one but the Arabs because Israel belonged to the Arabs in 1917. The British gave it to a group of Zionists who went to Palestine, ran the Palestinian Arabs out with terrorist groups, organized the state of Israel and did not get anywhere until Hitler came along and they swelled the state in 1948. That country belonged to the Palestinians. Not only that, they're moving to take over Egypt. Egypt is our motherland—it's in Africa.

We do not understand the concept of love. Here are a group of Zionists who come anywhere they want to organize love and feeling for a place called Israel, which was created in 1948, and their youth are willing to go and fight for Israel. Egypt belongs to us since four thousand years ago, and we sit here supporting the Zionists. We have got to be for the Arabs. Period.

That means that we also move with the rest of the Third World and understand exactly what is going on. It is no coincidence that the honky who stole a heart out of our brother and put it into another devil, was brought here on nationwide T.V. Now, for those of the older generation who say I may be harsh because I said the "devil," let me give you a biblical quotation: "Beware that the devil will come telling you that he can give you back life after death." If that's not what they're doing I don't know what it is.

Just today the United States voted for South Africa to come into the Olympics, and black people here are debating whether black athletes should be part of the Olympics. That is not a debate. The question is final. There can be no black athletes with any dignity participating in that white nonsense.

Survival means that we organize politically, we organize consciously (that's what they call education; we call it black consciousness, because that speaks to us, education speaks to them), we organize economically, and we organize militarily. If we don't do that, if you don't have a gun in your hand, they can snatch the ballot from you. But if you have a gun, it's either them or us. The preparation of that fight on all levels must become conscious among our people. We are ahead of the Jews in Germany because we know what they're getting ready to do. They tell us every day in their *Esquire* magazines, they tell us on their televisions, they tell us with the 15,000 soldiers they're putting in the cities, they tell us

123

with their tanks, they tell us with their Stoner guns,* they tell us! We must wake up and tell them *we* are going to get them.

Wipe the questions of minority and technology out of your mind. Technology never decides a war, it is the will of a people that decides a war. Wipe out of your mind the fact that we do not have guns. The Vietnamese didn't have guns when they started, now they have American guns, American tanks, American everything. If they come to get us they will have to bring some. We are going to take the gun, and the tank, and the grenade! Unless we raise our minds to the level of consciousness where we have an undying love for our people, where we're willing to shed our blood like Huey Newton did for our people, we will not survive. There are many people who know that. All of the brothers sitting on the stage,† all of the brothers around here [Black Panthers] know that when something goes down, we are the first ones offed. There's no question in any of our minds. Only thing going to stop us today is a bullet, and we are spittin' them back! The question is not whether or not we can move, but how this entire black community moves for survival in a world that's clearly heading for a color clash. That is what we must ask ourselves, the only question. We can do that only by organizing our people and orienting them toward an African ideology that speaks to our blackness—nothing else.

It's not a question of right or left, it's a question of black. You dig where we are coming from? We are coming from a black thing, from a *black* thing, that's where we are coming from. We can begin to pick up the threads of resistance that our ancestors laid down for us. And unless

* Special high-powered guns that can send bullets through brick walls ten feet thick; used as heavy duty police weapons.

† Rap Brown, Jim Forman, Chico Neblett, Bobby Seale, Eldridge Cleaver, Brother "Bunchy" Alprentice Carter (later killed during shoot-out on U.C.L.A. campus), and Ron Dellums.

we begin to understand our people as a people, we will not do that, because they *will* split us and divide us. That means consciously we have to begin to *organize our people!* Nothing else! We have no time for them; all our sweat, all our blood, even our life must go to our people, nothing else. We have to understand this consciously. Our youth must be organized with a revolutionary prospectus. A revolutionary prospectus says that we're fighting a war of liberation. In order to fight a war of liberation, you need an ideology of nationalism. We do not have this country. The nationalism can be nothing but black nationalism. It is insane to think of anything else. Black nationalism must be our ideology. While blackness is necessary, it is not sufficient, so we must move on to consciously organize our communities. And we recognize today while we're organizing that we do not have the money to feed our people, so there's no use saying, "Organize, we can get you a job." We can't get them, they control them, that is a fact. That isn't a reason for you to sit down, it is only more reason for you to fight. That's more of an inspiration to fight so you *can* give them a job rather than to sit down and say the honkies have us on every end. They are not God. We are a beautiful race of people, we can do anything we want to do; all we have to do is get up, get up, get up and do it!

We have to discuss very coldly the question of rebellions. It is a fact that they're prepared to meet rebellions anywhere in the cities. Now, what's going to happen if one of our brothers gets offed? What happens if they go ahead and off Huey Newton? We must develop tactics where we do the maximum damage to them with minor damage to us. When we move into the arena, that means that this black community must be organized if Brother Huey Newton goes, and ten honky cops go, won't a black man in this community get up and open his mouth, because if he does, *he* goes too. That means that in organizing for the maximum damage against them and minor damage to us, we must be consciously aware of the fact that there will be people in our community who are going around doing just that. In our community, we see nothing, we hear nothing, we know nothing. Now, the question of agents in our community is beginning to make us paranoid. We cannot become paranoid because what they can do is make us so afraid we won't move. So we're not going to do that. We're going to plan. Little groups will plan theirs, big groups will plan theirs. If an agent is found, there is no question; he is going to be offed in such a manner that any other black man who dares inform to the honky will have three thoughts before he even *talks* to a white man about reporting in our community.

Our people have demonstrated a willingness to fight. Our people have demonstrated the courage of our ancestors—to face tanks, guns, and police dogs with bricks and bottles. That is a courageous act! Since our people have demonstrated a willingness to fight, the question is how we can organize that fight so we win. If a major rebellion breaks out, our people may or may not become the losers, but if a small group was doing maximum damage, we remain on top. We remain on top. It is not a matter of *what* they might do, but only one of *how* and *when* they're going to do it. That is all. For us the question is not going to Vietnam any more, the question is how we can protect our brothers who do not go to Vietnam from going to jail so that when one brother says "Hell, no," there're enough people in that community around him, so that if they dare come in, they are going to face maximum damage in their community.

We are talking about survival. We are talking about a people whose entire culture, whose entire history, whose entire way of life have been destroyed. We're talking about a people who have produced in *this* year a generation of warriors who are going to restore to our people the humanity and the love that we have for each other. That's what we're talking about *today*, we are talking about becoming the executioners of our executioners. For example, you should give a lot of money to the Huey defense fund, because while some of that money will go for that court thing, the rest of the money's going for the executioners. If they execute Huey, the final execution rests in our hands.

It is simply a question of a people. They control everything. They make us fight, they make us steal, they judge us, they put us in prison, they parole us, they send us out, they pick us up again—where in God's name do we exercise any sense of dignity in this country? What in God's name do we control, except the church, whose ideology is set up to be compatible with the system that's against us? Where in God's name do we exercise any control as a people whose ancestors were the proudest people that walked the face of this earth? Everywhere the white man has gone he controls our people; in South Africa he steals the gold from our people, in the West Indies he steals the materials from our people, in South America, where he's scattered our people, he's raping us blind. He rapes us in America and in Nova Scotia. Where in God's name will we find a piece of earth that belongs to us so we can restore our humanity? Where will we find it unless this generation begins to organize to fight for it?

When this generation begins to fight, there can be no disruptive elements in our community. We will tolerate none. We put our lives on the line for anyone who fights for our people. Huey Newton fought for our people. Whether or not Huey Newton becomes free depends upon black people, nobody else. Other people may help, but the final decision on Brother Huey depends on *us*. He didn't lay down his life for other people, he laid it down for *us*. And if he did that, we must be willing to do the same, not only for him but for the generation that's going to follow us.

We must consciously organize every element in our

community. That work must begin. People must be willing to give money to an organizer who is willing to spend twenty-four hours a day organizing. He cannot organize from the poverty program because they tell him what to do. But if black people are giving him the money, he can do anything for the benefit of black people. We have to run all the exploiters out of our community. That means that people have to consciously give money, by any means necessary. Ask yourself, if you were white, why would you want to be a cop in a black ghetto today when you know they are looking for you? Why, if you weren't sick in the mind and felt you were so superior that you had the right to rule, why would you want a lousy $5,000-a-year job when you are white and you can make it in this society? Would you want to be in their community if they were ready to off you, for $4,000, for $5,000, for $6,000 a year? We have to understand the politics of those honkies in our community. They are there to patrol and to control. Well, we are going to do the patrolling and controlling. We are building a concept of peoplehood. If the honkies get in our way, they will have to go. We are not concerned about their way of life, we are concerned about our *people*. We want to give our people the dignity and humanity that we once knew as a people, and if they get in our way, they're going to be offed. We're not concerned with their system. Let them have it. We want our way of life, and we're going to get it. We're going to get it or nobody's going to have any peace on this earth.

I want to read a statement that Brother Huey P. Newton wrote yesterday when I saw him in jail:

> As the racist police escalate the war in our communities against black people, we reserve the right to self-defense and maximum retaliation.

All of the things we spoke about tonight centered around Brother Huey P. Newton because all of the things we spoke about tonight exemplify what he was trying to do. There is no need for us to go to jail today for what we *say*. They did that to Brother Malcolm X, they just offed him for what he was saying. We have to progress as a race. Brother Huey may or may not have wiped out that honky, but at least it shows a progression, at least we're not getting offed for what we say; we're getting offed for what we *do*. Understand this concept: when they offed Brother Malcolm, we did nothing; if they off Brother Huey, we *must* retaliate. Do you think that any other race of people will let them off somebody, and the rest of them sit there? Where in God's name would you find a race of people like that?

In the last five years we have lost some of our best leaders—Lumumba, Malcolm X, Brother Kwame Nkrumah—and we do nothing. While they are murdering our leaders, they take our youth and send them to Vietnam and Korea. We are slowly getting wiped out. We must retaliate, we must fight for our humanity. It is our humanity that is at stake. It is not a question of dollars and cents. We will survive, because we have survived what *they* couldn't survive—that's a natural-born fact. We have survived. We survived through slavery, we survived through the Depression, we survived through World War II, we survived after World War II when they threw us out of the jobs in the North, we survived their Korean War. We are going to survive. Ain't no doubt about that in my mind, no doubt at all.

Our problem is to develop an undying love for our people. We must be willing to give our talents, our sweat, our blood, even our life for our people. We must develop the concept that every Negro is a potential black man. You do not alienate your potential allies. Let's bring our people *home*. Let's bring our people *home*.

We must understand the concept that for us the question of community is not geography, it is a question of us black people, wherever we are. We have to consciously become a part of the 900 million black people that are separated over this world. We are separated by *them*. We are blood of the same blood and flesh of the same flesh. We do not know who is our sister, who is our brother, or where we came from. They took us from Africa and they put thousands of miles of water between us, but they forgot—blood is thicker than water. We are coming together. We are an African people with an African ideology, and we are wandering in the United States. We are going to build a concept of peoplehood in this country or there will be no country.

Brothers and sisters, Brother Huey P. Newton belongs to *us*. He is flesh of our flesh, he is blood of our blood. He may be Mrs. Newton's baby, but he is our brother. We do not have to talk about what we're going to do if we're consciously preparing and consciously willing to back those who prepare!

All we say: Brother Huey will be set free—or else!

10

The Black
American
and
Palestinian
Revolutions

I would like to begin by talking about the history of the black movement; as oppressed people we do have in common the fact that our press releases and our statements, if they even hit the news media, which is controlled by the oppressor, are often distorted and the press never tells the truth.

The truth is that the only course that black people in this country can take is a revolutionary path. As you know, African-Americans were stolen from Africa. We

Organization of Arab Students (O.A.S.) Convention, Ann Arbor, August 25–31, 1968.

131

were brought to this country as slaves. We had no choice as to whom we were to mate with, how we were to be mated, where we were to live, or anything. We had, of course, to face the most brutal oppression of anyone. Of the wretched of the earth, it is said the black people are the most damned. I am inclined to believe that because certainly we have faced the most brutal oppression. We have been stripped of everything. We have been the most dehumanized of all the oppressed people. Having been stripped of our culture, the black man now finds himself inside a country and inside a world that he must begin to try his best to relate to.

Now we find that black people in the United States are colonized people, as differentiated from exploited people. People who are exploited are oppressed people, so are colonized people. But exploited people are oppressed mainly for economic reasons. Colonized people are not only exploited because of economic wealth, but their culture, their values, their language, their entire way of life are stripped from them and they are forced to identify with the oppressor, and that's very important because it means that as the two groups that are oppressed move, the exploited and the colonized, they must move in different paths. For example, it is a fact that there are white people in this country who are exploited—they are not colonized. They may be stripped of their economic wealth, but they have the same values, the same culture, the same history and the same language as their rich white oppressor.

But now let us examine black people in this country. While we are also stripped of economic wealth and are poor, we are also stripped of our culture, our language, our history, and our very way of life. That, certainly, defines the difference between poor whites and black people in this country. And it differentiates around the world the difference between colonization and exploitation. We venture to say that colonization comes into play when there are people of a different race oppressing another race. Let me give a clear example. In Algeria today, French is taught; in the schools in Vietnam twenty years ago, French was taught, French was made the national language. In Algeria today, while Arabic is the national language, as the Algerians begin to cope with the process of de-colonization, they are still forced to use French in the upper grades. What it means is that the Algerians were stripped of their language. They were forced to speak the language of their oppressor. Once one is forced to speak the language of his oppressor, he begins to think that his oppressor is in fact superior and, by definition, his own way of life—his culture and his value system—is inferior. Is it not a fact that the Algerians who were to make it to the top had to, in fact, become Frenchmen? The same is true of the Vietnamese, and the same is true of the black Americans. If they want to be accepted by the oppressor they must, in fact, become carbon copies of their oppressor. I want to give that background because it is important for us to understand the movements in the world today. Let me give another example: it is a fact that the United States of America, which is the world's greatest imperialist power, does exploit Europe, but she exploits Europe economically. She colonizes the Third World—that is, the world of color—Asia, Africa and Latin America.

While 65 per cent of the French economy is underwritten by American businessmen, the French people can still speak their own language, they can still have their own type of culture. Let us take, for example, the island of Puerto Rico. The island of Puerto Rico, where over 85 per cent of the people speak English in their own schools in Puerto Rico for three years and Spanish for two years is, again, a question of race and the superiority complex of Western society built around an ingrained idea that because one is white, one is superior. So we say black people in America and perhaps colonized people around the world are not only fighting an economic system, but also a racist system. Black people in this country are fighting two evils. One of the evils is racism. The second is the evil of capitalism, or imperialism, which is the highest stage of capitalism. Since our fight is against those twin evils, we must prepare an ideology that will meet both of them—a society that is free of racism and a society that indeed is anti-capitalist and where capitalism cannot function. That is the goal of the black movement in this country. If those goals are not made clear, the movement will be subverted: we will find ourselves being black capitalists trying to enjoy a piece of the American pie, trying to identify with our oppressor and helping to oppress the rest of the world.

Now, there are a number of groups functioning in the black liberation movement in this country. I will not give the philosophy of those groups. I will not speak for them because I wouldn't want their representatives to speak for us. There are, of course, the National Association for the Advancement of Colored People, the Congress for Racial Equality, the Student Nonviolent Coordinating Committee, the Southern Christian Leadership Conference, and the Black Panther Party. Most of these groups have basically been fighting for a share of the American pie, at least until recently. That is to say, they were kept out of the American dream, and many of them thought that if they were to adopt the manners, the mode, the culture of the oppressor, they would be accepted and they too could enjoy the fruits of American imperialism. But today, among the young generation of blacks in this country, an ideology is developing that says we cannot, in fact, accept the system. This differentiates the black militant from the black revolutionary. The black militant is one who yells and screams about the evils of the American system, himself trying to become a part of that system. The black revolutionary's cry is not that he is excluded, but that he wants to destroy, overturn, and completely demolish the American system and start with a new one that allows humanity to flow. I stand, then, on the side of the black revolutionary and not on the side of the black militant. The word "revolution" is easily tossed around, and we become very confused. A revolution cannot begin until one seizes power. Let me give an example. Fidel Castro fought in the mountains for years—that was not the Cuban Revolution. The Cuban Revolution did not begin until Fidel Castro walked into Havana, drove out Batista and his American lackeys and said, "This day I claim this island for the masses of the Cuban people." Before the revolution, the revolutionary passes through a period that is called armed struggle when the revolutionary forces are engaged in battle against the forces that maintain the status quo. Around the world today, oppressed peoples are moving into the stages of armed struggle. Several are already in the stage of revolution—Cuba, China, and a few others. Black people in this country face a problem I don't know whether or not we will solve until in fact, if we are successful, we begin a revolution in this country.

Since we fight both racism and capitalism, we are not quite sure that merely because we have abolished capitalism and, let us say, set up either a state of socialism or communism, we will also automatically wipe out racism. Many people say that when you set up a socialist state you automatically destroy racism, but we are not quite sure of this, because of racist brutality in this country and our understanding of the theories of white supremacy. And while we try to cope with these problems we would have to ask the forces in the world that are fighting to liberate themselves from imperialism to maybe give us some time, because that's going to be a hard problem. For us, racism is more important, because we were made slaves by the racism ingrained in white people. They selected us because we were black. They had a number of white people they could choose from in their own continent, Europe, but they decided to come to Africa and for some reason pick on us. They say because we were physically superior!

Perhaps there is some truth to that, and we will see. If there is, we will soon find out.

For many black people in this country Fanon is becoming one of the men from whom we are gathering a lot of our ideological strength, and Fanon indeed is very important. He was sent to Algeria to work for the French. Everyone knows the history: he joined the liberation forces and was wounded, became a doctor for the liberation forces, went to Ghana representing the Algerian liberation government and began to write the profound book *The Wretched of the Earth*. Now, what Fanon says to us is precisely what we begin to know—that we must alienate ourselves from the values of the system we have been taught. That, of course, is a very difficult problem, especially for black people who live here and who are continually subjugated through propaganda.

A few years ago I was for the Jewish people of Israel. I wanted to know why the Arabs were bothering the Jews— I couldn't figure it out. It's not funny: most Americans believe that the Arabs are committing crimes against the Jews, because we live inside a society that postulates assertions and these assertions are accepted as truths and never questioned. Because of that, we find ourselves in a world of fog that makes it very difficult to move clearly, to find the correct ideology and the correct positions as we move. That becomes very important for a number of reasons. I want to touch on the problem of Zionism as we, black people of this country, see it, and what our relation must be to the Arab world and to the forces that are fighting against the Arab people.

Zionists have a very effective, offensive propaganda. They state their propaganda and everyone accepts it as the truth and they put on the defensive anyone who tries to even question their propaganda by calling him anti-Semitic. It's a very, very good trick: nobody wants to be anti-Semitic, nobody wants to hate people merely because of their race. The way we found to counteract the offensive propaganda of the Zionists is to state our propaganda, and state it offensively, and state ours as the truth, and not bow down or question or quibble with the Zionists' propaganda; that is the only way we have found to be able to deal with them. If the Zionists assert that they have a right to Israel, then we assert that the Palestinians have a right to Palestine. And once we assert that, there can be room for discussion. If we accept their assertion and we begin to quibble with the Zionists, there is never room for discussion. But once we assert that the Palestinians have a right to Palestine because it belongs to them, then there can be room for discussion in this country. That is precisely what we did: try very hard to calculate assertions that would for once put the Zionists on the defensive in this country and let them back up their so-called State of Israel, which we all know to be an unjust and certainly immoral state.

What makes the forces of Zionism so effective in their propaganda is that the Zionists have something else: not only do they assert theirs as a fact, and anyone who questions it they put on the defensive by calling him anti-Semitic, but the Zionists hook up the killing of six million Jews as a justification for the so-called State of Israel. They say: "Six million Jews were murdered by Hitler; we have a right to Israel." And that is a very dangerous thing. It is a fact that six million Jews were slaughtered by Hitler, but that six million Jews were murdered by Hitler does not give the Zionists the right to take Arab land. If the Zionists—I want to make sure I use the correct term because I don't want to be called anti-Semitic—if in fact the Zionists are worried that they have lost six million Jews in Germany, if they are worried about the treatment that Hitler meted out to them, then it seems clear to me that they should take the land for their home state from Germany, since it was Germany who fought them.

I think the reason why the so-called State of Israel gets

support from the Western powers is precisely because the role Israel is now playing was planned by the imperialists. I don't have to tell you the history, that when Balfour gave them the land it was totally impossible for them to get European Jews to move to Israel.* It was not until the slaughter of the Jews in Germany by Hitler that the State of Israel became a reality. Until then they could not get the state to move. No one would leave and no one would go. Who wanted to go to the desert, except Palestinians? This is a very important point in terms of our coming to grips and dealing with the propaganda of the Zionists. Because once you feel sorry and sympathetic with a person, then you give him leeway. And, of course, with the Zionists' propaganda telling people that there was nobody in Palestine—"It was a land without people for a people without land"—and making those assertions and propaganda into facts in the minds of our people, it becomes almost impossible to deal with it. Now we in this country, as a gesture of solidarity with our brothers in the Arab world, intend to deal with the Zionists for several reasons. *One reason is, the same Zionists that exploit the Arabs also exploit us in this country. That is a fact. And that is not anti-Semitic.*

Our propaganda must be offensive, we cannot just take a position of self-defense. That certainly can be related to physical combat. Che Guevara clearly states that self-defense does nothing but maintain the status quo. If one wants to change things, one must move against the status quo aggressively—that is a fact. And what the Zionists do is they have you believe that if you move aggressively

---

* In 1917, Lord Balfour bowed to Zionist pressure and declared that the British government was in favor of establishing a "national home" for the Jewish people in Palestine. The British government then contradicted that statement by adding that nothing should be done to damage the civil and religious rights of non-Jewish inhabitants of Palestine—the Arabs.

against them you are committing a criminal act. That's very clever.

We have watched their movement. What the Zionists do is they set up a state called Israel and then they give the justification for that state. People never question the foundations any more, or the beginnings, or the fact that the state came into being. As they expand after each war, the territory that they conquer becomes incorporated in the "State of Israel." No one questions that state any more, and they continue to expand. Always expanding, incorporating, expanding and incorporating. And anyone who tries to fight them becomes an "aggressor."

Now we stand clear—self-defense will only maintain the status quo. If Egypt, Syria, and Jordan took a position of self-defense today, they would come out losing because the Israelis still occupy their land. If they want the land back, they must move aggressively against the occupying forces. And as they move aggressively, we have to move aggressively. There is no need to talk about peaceful co-existence; anyone who calls for peaceful co-existence is calling for the status quo to remain the way it is. The only solution is armed revolution! Those who say that we can exist with the imperialist forces are saying that we can exist with things the way they are, we never have to change them. But if we are suffering, we need change; and we must decide how that change is to come about.

How then do we stand? We do not intend to discuss the internal policies of the Arab world, that's a discussion for the Arabs; we can only support the Arab world as we see fit. It is clear that we may have certain likes and we feel closer to certain groups or certain governments more than we do to the others. For example, we feel very close to the commandos in Palestine. We feel they are the group that will get most of our support.

We feel very strongly committed to those Arab countries that are arming their people, because if you are for the people you have nothing to fear from the people. We feel very strongly committed to those countries that are building revolutionary governments. And we are not afraid to say so. We know that the June 5th aggression had several purposes. One was to destroy the revolutionary governments of the Arab world, we know that. And so we will support those revolutionary governments in what little, meager way we can. Because the spreading of these revolutionary governments in the Arab world is indeed a threat to world imperialism.

Now then, what is our role as we see it, how can we work with our Arab brothers? Number one, we can begin to spread the propaganda against Zionism and begin to enlighten and educate the masses of our people. We have begun to do that. Not only did we do it publicly last year,* but at, for example, the National Convention of New Politics in Chicago last year, we have taken the position that *if white people who call themselves revolutionary or radical want our support, they have to condemn Zionism.* We will continue to do that when we work with groups—we must. We will continue to spread that. We're trying now in many of the black colleges across the country to see to it that Arab culture and the Arabic language become in fact a part of the curriculum so that we can begin to know more about the Arab way of life, and understand what the imperialists are doing. We intend to start story books and talk about life in the Arab world so that our people become aware and begin, as much as possible, to fight Zionist propaganda. The mass media of the United States of America, which wholeheartedly supports Israel, is unfortunately controlled by the Zionists. We intend to make it clear that we will help the struggle of the Arabs in any way we can, not only financially and morally, but with our very lives. We see Africa as our motherland.

* The reference is to SNCC's *Newsletter*, Summer 1967, which exposed Zionist tactics and terrorism in Palestine.

That's not so far-fetched. The Zionists built a propaganda that Palestine was the motherland, the homeland of the Jews. And building up this propaganda has made young Jewish people feel that they have to be committed to their homeland for life or death. When the aggression took place in 1967, millions of dollars were raised across America at the snap of a finger. Young Jewish people were dropping out of school to go and fight for the homeland. They established a state in 1948 and yet they feel such a strong tie with it. There is no difference in black people going to fight for and defend Egypt. Egypt is in Africa and Africa is our homeland. The oldest civilization in the world comes from Egypt. We must feel we are a part of it. There are many of us who are slowly beginning to prepare for that propaganda and prepare for the actual fight. We intend to fight imperialism wherever it is, in the United States or in our homeland. So we say very clearly that because Egypt is in our motherland, we will fight the forces of imperialism whenever they are trying to invade our homeland, and our motherland.

As we begin to develop our struggle more and more, there will be a lot of subversion. There will be a lot of setbacks. But we make clear now our position that we will never be intimidated by the United States of America, not any more. We, better than all the oppressed people of the world, know the United States—we have lived inside of her for four hundred years. No one has to tell us of her brutality, no one has to tell us of her exploitation, we know it better than anyone. In fact, we can tell you something about the United States of America's greatest mistake: unlike other empires, which colonized people on the people's own land, she had the gall to bring us out of our homeland and colonize us on land which belonged to someone else—after she had wiped out the Indians, of course.

We aim to fight with guns in our hands, we aim to fight to the death. The word surrender cannot exist for us. It is better for us to die on our feet at age twenty-six than to live in starvation and die at age seventy-six. We would rather die first. We will become the fifth column. They cannot stop us no matter how hard they try. Not only are we not going to the Vietnamese war, we say firmly and clearly that the North Vietnamese are our comrades-in-arms: they are fighting imperialism, we are fighting imperialism. We make it clear that we see the Arab world, not only as our brothers, but also as our comrades-in-arms. We are not worried about contradictions among the Arab countries. History and the oppressors' forces will force them to unite and to fight. They have no alternative; they must fight. Imperialism is like a sponge that is never satisfied until it has sucked up everything; in order just to live, the Arabs are going to have to fight. In order to live, we will have to fight.

The youth are going to lead their Arab world to victory. They're going to lead it as Fatima Bernawi* is doing. Yes, it is far better that every Arab woman become Fatima Bernawi and be wiped out than live under the shame that the Arab world now lives under. Yes, you should all become Lady Fatima.

This is the beginning of our ties, and we will strengthen them. We will work more closely with the Arab students wherever we can. Our eyes are now open: we have begun to see this trickery of Zionism; we have begun to see the evil of Zionism, and we will fight to wipe it out wherever it exists, in the Middle East or in the ghetto of the United States.

The United States is the greatest de-humanizer in the world, and Israel is nothing but a finger of the United States of America. It de-humanizes all over the world, and our fight today is a fight for humanity. It is not just a

---

* Fatima Bernawi, black Palestinian woman from Jerusalem, sentenced to life imprisonment by the Israeli occupation forces for her resistance activities as a member of Al Fatah.

fight to change systems, it is a fight for our very humanity, our freedom to live, to have the type of culture and language we desire, and to live and function and enjoy the wealth of the earth. Just as the Vietnamese are fighting for humanity, just as the Arab world is fighting for humanity, just as our forces in Africa are fighting for humanity, just as Latin Americans are fighting for humanity, the black man in America is fighting for humanity. We stand with the Third World. We don't care what the State Department says, we don't care what the C.I.A. says, we don't care what Lyndon Baines Johnson says, as long as we have legs they cannot stop us from going to Algeria. They cannot stop us from going to the United Arab Republic. They cannot stop us from going to Syria. As long as you invite us we will come. We are men. We will go where we want to go, learn what we want to learn, see what we want to see, talk with whom we want to talk, and fight with whom we want to fight. You invite us, we will come.

The world of humanity now turns; the oppressed are beginning to feel their strength. We are beginning to feel our power. It is in our unity that we will find victory, and we are not worried about unity; the contradictions, as I said before, will force that unity.

Now there are two dreams I have in my life. My dreams are rooted in reality, not in imagery. I dream, number one, of having coffee with my wife in South Africa; and number two, of having mint tea in Palestine.

11

A New
World
to Build

If we start with the fact that black people are a colonized people, we have to branch from there and see what other problems we have. We must then try and pose some of the solutions to those problems.

There are basically two levels on which a colonized people move when they begin to move for their liberation: one is called, for lack of a better term, entertainment, and the second is called education. Both of them are necessary.

The entertainment stage is very necessary. The entertainment is what's happening when black people say,

A & T University, Greensboro, North Carolina, December 9, 1968.

"We're going to burn this city down. We can get Whitey. He ain't that bad." It's a sort of entertainment—we're entertaining ourselves because, for the first time, we are publicly saying what we always privately felt but were afraid to say. And while we're saying it—even though we're not powerful enough to do what we say—it's a sort of catharsis, a necessity, because, until we get to the entertainment stage, we are psychologically unequal to our oppressor. After that stage, after we begin to feel psychologically equal to the oppressor, then comes the stage of strategic planning, working out a correct ideology for a cohesive force, and moving on to victory. Simple?

You've seen most of the entertainment on television; I think we've passed through that stage. Tonight I'd like to do as little entertainment as possible and as much education as possible, because in the final analysis it is the educational stage that is going to save us. I do not mean *school* education. I don't want you to think I mean becoming a doctor and lawyer and all of that. I think all of that has its place, but that is not the type of education I'm talking about. I'm talking about education that prepares us for a revolution so that we win.

As a colonized people we should look at some of the effects colonialism has on us. The major effect that colonialism has on any victim is that he, the victim, hates himself. Frantz Fanon points this out quite clearly in *The Wretched of the Earth*. Frantz Fanon—he was African, and he writes about us for a change. Everybody else is always writing about us.

We can easily point out symptoms that show our self-hatred for ourselves. For one, we're always quickly willing to fight each other. You go to a juke joint and a brother steps on your shoes: "Nigger, I'll kill you, you step on my shines." Walk down the streets of Greensboro, a white man steps on your shoes: "Yassuh, boss man." And while certainly the reason we do not attack the white man is because of fear, the proclivity, our wanting to attack the black man as readily as we do is because of a deep self-hatred, and when we see ourselves reflected in each other, we try to destroy each other. We try to destroy ourselves in self-hatred in many ways: brothers on the needle, wine addicts, the fights, gang wars, what have you—you can point to so many ways we try to destroy ourselves.

Even deeper than that, the self-hatred is a result of something more subtle. As victims of colonialism we try to identify with the oppressor on every level we can. We want to be like the white people who oppress us in this country, and since we want to be like them we hate ourselves because they hate us. Understand that? And we want the oppressor to define everything for us. They define what education is, they define what work is, they define how we move, what we do, and how we look—the oppressor defines even the standards of beauty for the victims of colonialism. You should be aware that in colonialism, race comes into play, and you have colonialism when one race is oppressing another race. And so what you have is the victim, the race that's colonized, trying to look like his oppressors; that's why all of our women use hot combs and fry their hair. It is done because we psychologically want to be like white people. We deny it—we couldn't admit it to ourselves consciously. But subconsciously we try to be like white people, and white people want it that way. That's why there is nothing positive about black people in their books, in their literature—in any of their mass communication, only negative things are seen about black people. The positive images are white folks. And we try to identify with the positive images. Even if the positive images are beating us up!

You dig Tarzan? You used to go to the movies and yell for Tarzan to beat up your ancestors. "Here, Tarzan, get that nigger. Look out for that black savage!" What we were doing, we were psychologically identifying with Tarzan, a white man, who was beating up us Africans.

We tried to identify with white people so much that we refused to admit that we had anything to do with Africa. It is deeply important to understand this concept of self-hatred if we are going to survive. If we're even going to live long enough to get a cohesive ideology for our people, it is a basic necessity that we understand that self-hatred. In order to counteract this self-hatred, we have a new concept that we are trying to throw out around the country—it is: for our people, black people, we must have undying love.

Undying love is very hard, especially for those of us who hate ourselves and don't recognize it. We try to get out of it: you know, you see cats who call themselves black nationalists or revolutionaries; they get a bad afro and run around campus, they don't talk to anybody. You see, they think they've made it, but they do not recognize how much self-hatred is working on them because they still hate their brothers so much that they don't even communicate with them and try to show them where it's at. Very important, undying love.

Our people have demonstrated undying love. The white man doesn't want us to know that, but we don't take the white man's interpretations here. If you're walking down the street and you have undying love for your brother and a policeman shoots him and you try to kill that policeman with a brick, a bottle, a stick—anything you have in your hand—that *is* undying love. When you reach the stage of undying love, one forgets what is called "reason." If you see a policeman hitting your mama, you ain't got time for no reason, you're going to try to kill him. And if we saw every black woman as our mother, then we would begin to understand this concept of undying love. If we saw every black man as our brother, then we would begin to understand this concept of undying love. And if we saw every black woman as our sister, then we would understand this concept of undying love. It is that concept, first and most important, that we must try to achieve.

Undying love does not mean only that you're willing to die for your people, it also means you're willing to kill for your people—which is more important. And please don't get excited with the word "kill," because all of the young men in here are asked to kill for this country. When they send you to Vietnam they don't send you just to die, they send you to kill. And if you can kill for a country that's done what it has to us for all these years, it should certainly be easy for you to kill for your people.

There's another concept we're trying to put out around the country: every Negro is a potential black man. This concept is not only necessary, it is revolutionary, as I hope to explain as we move along. Now, before we go into the process of the Negro becoming a black man, we ought to differentiate between the current Negro and the current black man, because it is very confusing. When we were in Africa—you know we came from Africa, don't you? Don't laugh. Really. You know, you ask anybody on campus: "Hey, man, where are you from?" "Dallas." "Say, where's your mother from?" "Dallas." "Where's your grandfather from?" "Charleston." "And where's your great-grandfather from?" "Ummm." "You don't know where your great-grandfather's from?" "Ummm." "Nigger, he's from Africa. You know it. Stop lying."

When we were in Africa we were called Africans or blacks; when we were in Africa we were free. When we were captured and stolen and brought to the United States, we became Negroes. So negro is synonymous with slavery. Before slavery, there were no Negroes; once you set foot on the United States, the borders of the United States, and you set foot as a slave, you became a Negro. So if you say you're a Negro, what you're saying is that your beginning is in slavery. If your beginning is in slavery, the best you can hope to be is a good slave. And you can see it all the time. You know the soul stations; they do the Negro news spot every half hour or so. They say, for example, "Even though Benjamin Banneker was in slavery he worked very hard to help George Washington lay out the city of Washington and cross the Delaware River." Now does that make sense to you? Your people in slavery, and you're going to help the white man build a stronger country! You got to be a Negro to do that. A black man would turn the boat over while Washington was in the river Delaware, because the first thing in his mind is his liberation—not serving any country. That's what all those Negro news spots ought to say. "Even though he was a slave he did such and such; even though he's a Negro who is a second-class citizen he's still trying to do such and such." Look here—if I'm in a country and my brothers and sisters are in slavery, I'm going to try and tear that country up. Rip it up, capture it. The concept of Negro and black man becomes important, 'cause if you're a Negro you can only hope to be a Benjamin Banneker—or a George Washington Carver, even though he did give us the peanut or a Charles Drew, who died on a highway because they wouldn't give him white blood plasma, though he invented blood plasma; when he got in an accident and needed blood, white folk wouldn't give him blood even though he was saving their lives. I wouldn't want to help anybody who's enslaving me and my people. We must be black. If we are black, then we can trace our ancestry back to Africa, and we can begin to learn about the warriors in Africa who killed white folk. And I mean kill—a whole lot, like Cetswayo, Hannibal, Moshesh, Menelik, Lobenguela and all those cats.

There are some who say, "Well, we're the black Americans." Junk. You ain't nothing but an African, and you ain't had nothing to say about where you were born; the white man decided where you would be born, when you would be born, and how you would be born. For us to keep talking this junk about "We're Americans first"—that's junk. We're Africans. We happened to be born in America because the white man needed us there, and that's the only reason why. That does not make you an American, incidentally. It makes you a tool of America. Why, then, do we say that every Negro is a potential black man? Because in every black man in America there is a Rap Brown. The white man knows that; that's why he's got to get rid of Rap Brown. In every black man there's a Huey P. Newton, an Eldridge Cleaver, a LeRoi Jones, a Rap Brown, because the conditions that produced Rap Brown, Huey Newton and Eldridge Cleaver are the same conditions we all live in. And we say that because we have to give our people time to wake up. Too many times our brothers who become nationalists, our sisters who get afros, they turn their backs overnight on the brothers and sisters who need them the most. I hope you don't get upset when I imply that you fry the hair. But I only do it, really, because my mother told me you only fry dead things, and so I don't understand how the women must fry their hair, because I think their hair is alive—unless they're saying in order to look like white folks your hair has got to be dead. We say that every Negro is a potential black man because if we're talking about unity we have to believe that it is possible for all of us to be united. We say every Negro is a potential black man because when Brother Malcolm X was speaking a lot of us were saying, "I wish that nigger would shut up talking about all this hate, killing and violence." We won't admit it, today, but a whole lot of us said, "I wish he'd shut up all this preaching hate and this nonsense about black, black, black." We didn't like it when he was around. Just like it took time for Brother Malcolm to wake some of us up, it's gonna take time for those of us who are awake now to wake the others up. And if we have an undying love for our people, we are willing to take the time and patience with them.

Too many times, whenever a revolutionary group gets on campus, their first attack is on Uncle Tom. "Hey, let's get together. We've got to get that Uncle Tom before we get going." There's nothing new about that, nothing, nothing—niggers have always been fighting niggers. Just because they say it's for a revolutionary reason does not make them revolutionary: they're still fightin' niggers, still doing it. It's that self-hatred still there. How can a man talk about killing an Uncle Tom when honky cops are running rampant in our community? In the Party we say: Before you talk about killing an Uncle Tom, kill five white cops, then we will respect your talk about killing an Uncle Tom. But before you kill somebody white, don't talk about killing anybody black. Every Negro is a potential black man.

The third concept is perhaps the most difficult, but we're going to have to take time with it because it is a basic necessity if we're going to achieve success in the confrontation that *I* believe is going to come anyway, whether we like it or not. For us, black people, the question of community is not simply a question of geographical boundaries but it is also a question of our people and where we are. Example: if you went to New York you would not feel as if you were part of the community until you got to Harlem. If you went to Los Angeles you would not feel part of our community until you got to Watts. If you went to Chicago, the West Side; Washington, D.C., the whole city. But this concept is not only for the United States but, more important, on an international level—which is what we must begin to talk about.

We are Africans. We are scattered all over the Western Hemisphere; black people can be found from South Africa to Nova Scotia. Fifty per cent of the population in Brazil: black. In Panama, in Guatemala, in the Dominican Republic, in the West Indies, in the United States, in Canada—we're all over. And we are the same people. But now what happens is, if we happen to be born in the United States, the man says, "You are an American." If you happen to be born in Brazil, the man says, "You're a Brazilian." So if America and Brazil go to war, niggers will be fighting niggers once again—only one is an American nigger and the other's a Brazilian nigger. And if we are to move on an international level to stop the fighting that the man is going to try to develop inside our communities, we must now begin to develop an international perspective which says that we are Africans wherever we are and we will never fight another African. If white folks got a fight with Brazil, let the white folk in America and the white folk in Brazil fight. When they finish, we'll fight the winners and keep the land.

That concept must be developed more and more, because the way the white man moves is to divide people against people so they fight themselves. Witness North Korea versus South Korea, North Vietnam versus South Vietnam. Now here these people have been living together all their lives. All of a sudden the white man comes along and says, "You North Vietnamese, you South Vietnamese; you communists, you democratic; you hate each other—fight!" And if the good guys are winning, he calls in the niggers. "Nigger, go fight for democracy in Vietnam." "Yassuh." Witness Africa: Nigeria, Biafra. When the white man gets ready to move, he divides. And if we're going to move ahead of him we must move so that when he tries to divide he will not be able to do it. Therefore we must begin to understand those three concepts. (1) We must have an undying love. We must have an undying love for our people. (2) Every Negro is a potential black man. (3) For black people the question of community is not simply a question of geographical boundaries but a question of our people and where we are.

Now we've all come to the decision—or, let's say that white folk have finally admitted—that racism is an institution in America. They've just admitted it. As if they just discovered it. Every time you talk about racism they say, "The Kerner Report says so." Rap Brown told them that three years before the Kerner Report was written. They have to give legitimacy to themselves. Well, America is racist, even the Kerner Report admits it. Very white of the Kerner Report to do that.

If a society is racist, the educational system must perpetuate racism. Education, says Frantz Fanon, is the reestablishment and the reinforcement of values and institutions of a given society. So in any school you go to in America, you're going to a racist school and getting a racist education. Let me give you an example . . . I don't know, did you have reading comprehension? Did you have a reading comprehension test in the South? We did in the North. You know reading comprehension: you read a paragraph and answer the questions they ask you. Right. You know when you were in the first grade you used to read 'em and you'd answer all the questions; you got to tenth grade and you ran home and you said, "Hey, Ma, I'm reading tenth-grade level," and she'd say, "Boy, you smart." Well, go back and look at what you were reading. The paragraph will say: "The best political system in the world is the two-party system. That's been proven time and time again. It's the most stable, most equitable, most fundamental, blah blah blah blah blah." And they ask you down at the bottom, "What's the best system in the world?" You pass if you answer, "Two-party system." Imagine that.

Read another one. "Abraham Lincoln was a good man. In order to become President he worked hard, studied well, and believed in freedom, democracy, blah blah blah, never stole." "George Washington never told a lie, therefore he became President." "Why did George Washington become President?" "Because he never told a lie." You didn't recognize that while you thought you were being smart they were brainwashing you—or rather should I say whitewashing you—with what they wanted you to know. All this time we thought we were very smart, but what we were doing was just reading and giving back to the white man what he wanted us to give back to him: positive images of white Western society, negative images of every other society, and the most negative of all the negatives, black people. It is totally impossible for a real black university to function inside a white state. It cannot happen. Here's an example: at Columbia University, the black-studies people hire a black course adviser. They never question whether they need a black one, but because the white boy has one, and they're into "equality," they think they also need one. It is intellectual laziness. And it is accepting, once again, the oppressors' values and institutions without recognizing it, because when black students set up black studies programs they never question the underlying assumptions of education, which we must begin to question here tonight.

The first one is a question of methodology and ideology. Black people cannot have the same ideology that white people have and call that education. Yet black students, when they set up black courses, accept the same ideology as white folk, so what you have is what my friend Chico Neblett of Boston calls "a black carbon copy of a white ideology." People think this is black, and it is not.

Also, because we accept wholeheartedly the methodology of white racist society without questioning it, the languages probably taught at this school are probably European languages—French, Spanish, Latin, English, German, that kind. You may be lucky and have Chinese. And you *may* be lucky and have been able to get a course in an African language. But if we were to get an African language at this course the teacher who teaches that African language would probably teach it the same way a white teacher teaches French or a black teacher teaches French; he would accept the same methodology. He does not even question the methodology. What the teacher, and the student, fail to realize is that the methodology is suited to the ideology—which leads us to our second group of problems around education: technological development versus human development.

In Western society the decision has been made, they want technological development before human development—isn't that clear? They decided to get the atomic bomb, to get an industrial society—at the expense of human development. If we are to talk about real, new types of education among black people, we must see whether or not technical development has to be at the expense of human development. And if it does, then we ought to say that we would rather have human development than technical development. But that is too profound for most of us to even understand, and it scares us, because what we try to do is keep up with the white man rather than set our own pace, and we don't even recognize that though we say we are black. When he ends the book, *The Wretched of the Earth*, Fanon says that friends, brothers, sisters should come together. We have a new world to build. Our object is not to catch up with Europe. Four hundred years ago a colony tried to catch up with Europe. She succeeded so well that today the United States of America is the monster of the world. Come, brothers and sisters, let us not try to catch up with Europe. Let us try to go forward in the company of man. All men. Fanon is telling us that we can't waste our time trying to catch up with this man because we might develop atomic bombs and have our zombies just like him. Or we may become as cold as he has become because of the desires to become technologically advanced. So before we even talk about education, we must question whether or not we want those things; we should question whether or not a university, where all the people come and are taught, is really the best way to teach. All those things have to be questioned if we are, in fact, serious about what we're doing. A university is geared for mass production, and we should decide whether or not we want to mass-produce our people—their education, that is.

Because we are afraid to venture out and create for ourselves the new types of things that we have to think about, we stay where we are and imitate the white boy. If they want to bring a course to A&T they say, "Let's see how Harvard did it." We don't want a black Harvard, we don't want a black Columbia, we don't want a black Yale. We want colleges that serve the basic needs and desires of the masses of our people.

Now all of that is said to show you that if you talk about revolution, as do most people in the country today, you don't understand what you're talking about. We should begin to define those terms that are so loosely thrown around all across the country.

Let us understand violence, because that's very important. There is always violence. Now what happens is that the oppressor, because he has power, can institutionalize and legitimitize his violence to the point where we, the oppressed, accept it. Because the oppressed does not have the power to institutionalize his violence, his violence is always seen very quickly as illegitimate.

You do not think it is violent to kill in Vietnam because you get a medal. You're defending the "free world" against communism. You don't know what communism is; if it hit you upside your face you wouldn't know what to do with it, but that's what you're fighting against, and you don't even consider that violence. The only type of violence you see is the violence directed against the oppressor, because the oppressor wants it that way. What, then, is revolutionary violence?

Revolutionary violence is that violence that seeks to overthrow an established system that serves a few people, to establish a new system that serves the masses of our people. The other type of violence, counterrevolutionary violence, seeks to maintain in power an established form or an established system that serves a few people. In America, the police would come under counterrevolutionary violence. And those people who are blowing up police stations and machine-gunning police stations and shooting policemen would be considered under the topic of revolutionary violence. In Vietnam, the American forces and the puppets in South Vietnam would be counterrevolutionary violence. The Viet Cong would be revolutionary violence. So we are *for* revolutionary violence. I'd rather see a brother kill a cop than kill a Vietnamese. At least he's got reason for killing the cop. When you kill a Vietnamese, you're a hero; you don't even know why you kill him; at least if you kill a cop you're doing it for a reason. It's better to kill with passion than to kill passionless.

Now the term "revolution" is thrown around very loosely *because* the white man wants that. Stuff about "the black revolution"—the revolution isn't going on now. A revolution occurs only after you have seized power, because a revolution means revolutionizing, changing, and you can't change anything before you have power.

The period preceding the revolution is a period of "armed struggle," when the revolutionary forces are fighting the counterrevolutionary forces. In this country, America, black people have just begun to scratch the surface of armed struggle. If we're talking about true revolution in this country, we're talking about a fight of a generation. This generation. Revolution will not come tomorrow, two years from now, five years from now, ten years from now. We are talking about a generation of young black people willing to fight and give their lives for a revolution that will benefit the generations who come after us. And we have to understand that. We're too loose with the term "revolution," but if we begin to understand that, then we will really know what revolution is. And if we don't define it for ourselves, the white man will define it, tell us we had a revolution and we're free. Don't laugh—he did that, he used to tell us: "Get the vote and be free." Remember when they used to run around and say, "Well, when the Voting Rights Act is passed you will be free." Or was it "Free in '63." You remember. "Free in '63"? After the Voting Rights Acts passed, white folks said, "Niggers, you're free." That's what they did after slavery. We said "Yassuh, we free. Thank you." And then they had to pass the 13th, 14th, and 15th. So they passed the 13th, and then they said, "Niggers, you're free." "Yassuh. Thank you." They came back a little bit later, passed the 14th and 15th and said, "Niggers, you're free." "Yassuh. Thank you." Every time they define for us we're free, we believe them and we sit down. We must define for ourselves when we are truly free. And only we can do that.

Now I want to make a distinction between a black militant and a black revolutionary. They're very confusing because at first they look alike. A black militant is an angry black man—notice I didn't say Negro—who is angry at white folks for keeping him out of their system. You see them all the time. You know, they find out maybe the city's getting tense, they've got their afros and dashikis, they run down the street. You see them on the news, having a press conference on the corner. "If the man don't give us a poverty program, this city is going to go; it's going to follow Detroit, it's going to follow Washington." All of a sudden they're on television every day, telling the mayor, "Mr. Mayor, this city will burn. I know the feeling of the people in the ghetto. I rub shoulders with them. I know their alienation. I know their sense of dejection. I know this; I know that; and the city will go." The mayor puts them on a committee and gives them a $30,000-a-year job, then the city blows and they run down the street: "Cool it, brothers, we got dialogue with the mayor."

But a black revolutionary is an angry young man who wants to tear down and destroy an entire system that is oppressing his people and replace it with a new system where his people can live like human beings.

This country is crawling with black militants, but there

are very few black revolutionaries. We need more black revolutionaries and less militants. The militant, in the final analysis, is a man who is concerned only about himself, and he uses the feelings of his people to advance himself. That's the worst crime you can commit.

Sometimes the people believe in this black man who runs around yelling about what's going to happen if he don't get a job on the mayor's committee, they really do. Then, when he gets that $30,000 job, they say, See how jive that nigger is? This country's going to use more and more black militants, you watch how they use them. One actor brother points out that on every television show where they got black people now, he's a cop. Think of that. Every black male in it—he's a cop. Even *The Outcast.* He's a bounty hunter. Now, he's a bad dude. He beats up white folk, and he even kills a few. But he's still a cop. *NYPD,* he's a cop; *Mission Impossible,* he's a cop; *I Spy,* he's an international cop. What they're doing to us is they're trying to make us identify with a black man who fights for law and order—*their* law, and *their* order. Notice, if you will, finally, how racism works: on every program where there's a white family and somebody is missing, the mother is missing: there's always a male image present. But on a "black" program the father is missing, and once again there is a matriarchal system. Here we have all these black people looking at *Julia,* and swearing that's being black, and that's being nothing but nigger. "Do you watch *Julia?* Ain't she good; she got a whole new show. Yeah. And her husband died in Vietnam." It is so difficult to be black in this society. Sometimes we Tom without even knowing it, that's true. We must begin to analyze carefully where we're going. There can never be a true black series on television because a true black series will have to deny everything they call American. It will have to. Can they ever deny what they are and give us television space for it? They can't. The *Mod Squad* is supposed to be so bad. Right on. Got this nigger with an afro getting up there talking about, "Well actually, you know, we shouldn't fight and kill"—now he's a *cop*. "We shouldn't fight and kill; we should go to school and study hard and get a good education and become a cop like me and work off-duty for *Mod Squad*." Now all of us try and identify with this vain attempt. You have to be careful: white folk have not improved—they've been gettin' smarter.

Now, we want to move into the international scene a little because it's very important. And we ought to start with the Middle East. Because a lot of us are confused about the Middle East, you see. And we have to understand who our allies will be around the world. Our ally cannot be Israel; it must be the Arabs. You have to understand that, but you don't understand it because you don't think it's important. It is important because the so-called State of Israel was set up by white people who took it from the Arabs. And when they were first looking for a spot of land they were going to take it from Uganda, which is in our motherland, Africa. And they were going to give to the Jews a part of Africa! So you got to understand that. Secondly, at this point in history the so-called State of Israel, which was set up in 1948, is occupying land in Egypt. Did you know Egypt was in Africa? How could you be for Israel? They're occupying the land of our birth. The land of our ancestors. But because we do not know, we go around talking about "we should support Israel." Because they've whipped a game on us. They tell us that six million Jews were killed during Hitler's time—and they were. But then they tell us because six million Jews were killed the Jews have a right to land in the Middle East. Nigger, a hundred million niggers been killed during the trip from Africa to America. What land do we have? What land do we have? They tell us that the death of six million Jews justifies the taking of the land in the Middle East. Hitler killed six million Jews; the Arabs didn't touch the hair of one Jew. If Hitler killed six million Jews, Hitler lost the war, to the victor belong the spoils, take the land from Germany; leave the Middle East alone. We have got to understand everyday international politics.

We want to talk about Africa, because it is important. It is important because we do not know *anything* about our mother continent. For example, guerrilla warfare has been going on for seven years in over four countries in Africa. We don't even know the names of those countries. Guinea-Bissau, which is on the west coast, controlled by the Portuguese; Mozambique, in southeast Africa; Angola, in southwest Africa; South West Africa, which is of course in southwest Africa; Zimbabwe—that's what the white folks call Rhodesia after Cecil Rhodes who stole our country and named it after himself. We have to begin to understand Africa because we must begin to relate to Africa on all levels. The white man wants us to relate to Africa, but only culturally. He does not want us to relate to Africa politically or economically. Because in that lies his death. He talks about Africa, but he only shows you what people wear in Africa. He doesn't talk about the concrete political systems in Africa, nor does he talk about the concrete economical systems in Africa. He wants us to relate to Africa only on a cultural level. And we *must* begin to understand it on a political and economic level. So that we can begin to know where to fight, when to fight, and who to fight.

Now, let me say one thing before I sit down. A lot of people say that Rap Brown, Eldridge Cleaver, Huey Newton—all these young leaders preach hate. Well that's not necessarily true. There are two types of philosophies in the world: there is metaphysical philosophy and there is dialectic philosophy. Metaphysical philosophy is archaic. I don't want to waste time with that. As students, you should know that. Now dialectical philosophy is the one that deals with opposites. It says that for every action there is a reaction, and every emotion has an opposite emotion, etc. For example: for hot there's cold; for wet there's dry; for laughter, tears; boy, girl; white, black— they're opposites. We live in a world of opposites. And dialectic philosophy says that the way the world changes is when these opposites react with each other, they polarize. Now, a lot of people say, "I don't hate folks; you're not supposed to hate." Well, if you don't hate you can't love—unless you're only one-sided. But if you agree that you live in a world of dialectics, then if you love you must at least have the capacity to hate. And you must *know* hate in order to differentiate love. You have a continuum of love—like—get along with—O.K.—obnoxious—dislike—hate. Now I know people tell you all the time there's no such thing as hate. That's not true. If there's no such thing as hate, then there's no such thing as love. People say that we talk about hate. Let me give you a concrete example. When Dr. King died, eight o'clock at night we hit the streets, you know. And I thought, "Oh, man! This city is goin' to burn." And someone said, "Oh, man, where you going? Watcha gonna do?" I said, "They gonna tear this city up. Period." He said, "Don't do that. Don't do that." I said, "Yeah, they gonna get 'em all." "No, don't do that. Why are you all so full of hate?" He said, "I ain't got no hate." I said, "You don't hate nobody?" He says, "No, I don't hate nobody." I said, "After what they did to Dr. King?" He said, "No, I don't hate 'em." I said, "You don't hate 'em because you never did *love* Dr. King. Because if you loved Dr. King, if you love black people, you would have to hate the enemies of black people. If you don't hate their enemies you don't love your people."

If you have children, and somebody comes to destroy your children, you try to kill that somebody because you love your children. You don't sit there and talk, "I don't hate." If you have a sister, or a brother, and somebody's trying to rape your sister or kill your brother, you try to kill them because you love your sister and your brother. You love your sister and your brother. It is not that we hate America so much; it is only that we love our people more.

12

The
Pitfalls
of
Liberalism

Whenever one writes about a problem in the United States, especially concerning the racial atmosphere, the problem written about is usually black people, that they are either extremist, irresponsible, or ideologically naïve.

What we want to do here is to talk about white society, and the liberal segment of white society, because we want to prove the pitfalls of liberalism, that is, the pitfalls of liberals in their political thinking.

Whenever articles are written, whenever political

Privately printed under the direction of Jean Farrow and Cleveland L. Sellers, January, 1969.

speeches are given, or whenever analyses are made about a situation, it is assumed that certain people of one group, either the left or the right, the rich or the poor, the whites or the blacks, are causing polarization. The fact is that conditions cause polarization, and that certain people can act as catalysts to speed up the polarization; for example, Rap Brown or Huey Newton can be a catalyst for speeding up the polarization of blacks against whites in the United States, but the conditions are already there. George Wallace can speed up the polarization of whites against blacks in America, but again, the conditions are already there.

Many people want to know why, out of the entire white segment of society, we want to criticize the liberals. We have to criticize them because they represent the liaison between both groups, between the oppressed and the oppressor. The liberal tries to become an arbitrator, but he is incapable of solving the problems. He promises the oppressor that he can keep the oppressed under control; that he will stop them from becoming illegal (in this case illegal means violent). At the same time, he promises the oppressed that he will be able to alleviate their suffering— in due time. Historically, of course, we know this is impossible, and our era will not escape history.

The most perturbing question for the liberal is the question of violence. The liberal's initial reaction to violence is to try to convince the oppressed that violence is an incorrect tactic, that violence will not work, that violence never accomplishes anything. The Europeans took America through violence and through violence they established the most powerful country in the world. Through violence they maintain the most powerful country in the world. It is absolutely absurd for one to say that violence never accomplishes anything.

Today power is defined by the amount of violence one can bring against one's enemy—that is how you decide how powerful a country is; power is defined not by the number of people living in a country, it is not based on the amount of resources to be found in that country, it is not based upon the good will of the leaders or the majority of that people. When one talks about a powerful country, one is talking precisely about the amount of violence that that country can heap upon its enemy. We must be clear in our minds about that. Russia is a powerful country, not because there are so many millions of Russians but because Russia has great atomic strength, great atomic power, which of course is violence. America can unleash an infinite amount of violence, and that is the only way one considers America powerful. No one considers Vietnam powerful, because Vietnam cannot unleash the same amount of violence. Yet if one wanted to define power as the ability to do, it seems to me that Vietnam is much more powerful than the United States. But because we have been conditioned by Western thoughts today to equate power with violence, we tend to do that at all times, except when the oppressed begin to equate power with violence—then it becomes an "incorrect" equation.

Most societies in the West are not opposed to violence. The oppressor is only opposed to violence when the oppressed talks about using violence against the oppressor. Then the question of violence is raised as the incorrect means to attain one's ends. Witness, for example, that Britain, France, and the United States have time and time again armed black people to fight their enemies for them. France armed Senegalese in World War II, Britain of course armed Africa and the West Indies, and the United States always armed the Africans living in the United States. But that is only to fight against *their* enemy, and the question of violence is never raised. The only time the United States or England or France will become concerned about the question of violence is when the people whom they armed to kill their enemies will pick up those arms against them. For another example, practically every country in the West today is giving guns either to

Nigeria or to Biafra. They do not mind giving those guns to those people as long as they use them to kill each other, but they will never give them guns to kill another white man or to fight another white country.

The way the oppressor tries to stop the oppressed from using violence as a means to attain liberation is to raise ethical or moral questions about violence. I want to state emphatically here that violence in any society is neither moral nor is it ethical. It is neither right nor is it wrong. It is just simply a question of who has the power to legalize violence.

It is not a question of whether it is right to kill or it is wrong to kill; killing goes on. Let me give an example: if I were in Vietnam, if I killed thirty yellow people who were pointed out to me by white Americans as my enemy, I would be given a medal. I would become a hero. I would have killed America's enemy—but America's enemy is not my enemy. If I were to kill thirty white policemen in Washington, D.C., who have been brutalizing my people and who are my enemy, I would get the electric chair. It is simply a question of who has the power to legalize violence. In Vietnam our violence is legalized by white America. In Washington, D.C., my violence is not legalized, because Africans living in Washington, D.C., do not have the power to legalize their violence.

I used that example only to point out that the oppressor never really puts an ethical or moral judgment on violence, except when the oppressed picks up guns against the oppressor. For the oppressor, violence is simply the expedient thing to do.

Is it not violent for a child to go to bed hungry in the richest country in the world? I think that is violent. But that type of violence is so institutionalized that it becomes a part of our way of life. Not only do we accept poverty, we even find it normal. And that again is because the oppressor makes his violence a part of the functioning society. But the violence of the oppressed becomes disruptive. It is disruptive to the ruling circles of a given society. And because it is disruptive it is therefore very easy to recognize, and therefore it becomes the target of all those who in fact do not want to change the society. What we want to do for our people, the oppressed, is to begin to legitimatize violence in their minds. So that for us violence against the oppressor will be expedient. This is very important, because we have all been brainwashed into accepting questions of moral judgment when violence is used against the oppressor.

If I kill in Vietnam I am allowed to go free; it has been legalized for me. It has not been legitimatized in my mind. I must legitimatize it in my own mind, and even though it is legal I may never legitimatize it in my own mind. There are a lot of people who come back from Vietnam, who have killed where killing was legalized, but who still have psychological problems over the fact that they have killed. We must understand, however, that to legitimatize killing in one's mind does not make it legal. For example, I have completely legitimatized in my mind the killing of white policemen who terrorize black communities. However, if I get caught killing a white policeman, I have to go to jail, because I do not as yet have the power to legalize that type of killing. The oppressed must begin to legitimatize that type of violence in the minds of our people, even though it is illegal at this time, and we have to keep striving every chance we get to attain that end.

Now, I think the biggest problem with the white liberal in America, and perhaps the liberal around the world, is that his primary task is to stop confrontation, stop conflicts, *not* to redress grievances, but to stop confrontation. And this is very clear, it must become very, very clear in all our minds. Because once we see what the primary task of the liberal is, then we can see the necessity of not wasting time with him. His primary role is to stop confrontation. Because the liberal assumes a priori that a confrontation is not going to solve the problem. This, of course, is an incorrect assumption. We know that.

We need not waste time showing that this assumption of the liberals is clearly ridiculous. I think that history has shown that confrontation in many cases has resolved quite a number of problems—look at the Russian revolution, the Cuban revolution, the Chinese revolution. In many cases, stopping confrontation really means prolonging suffering.

The liberal is so preoccupied with stopping confrontation that he usually finds himself defending and calling for law and order, the law and order of the oppressor. Confrontation would disrupt the smooth functioning of the society and so the politics of the liberal leads him into a position where he finds himself politically aligned with the oppressor rather than with the oppressed.

The reason the liberal seeks to stop confrontation—and this is the second pitfall of liberalism—is that his role, regardless of what he says, is really to maintain the status quo, rather than to change it. He enjoys economic stability from the status quo and if he fights for change he is risking his economic stability. What the liberal is really saying is that he hopes to bring about justice and economic stability for everyone through reform, that somehow the society will be able to keep expanding without redistributing the wealth.

This leads to the third pitfall of the liberal. The liberal is afraid to alienate anyone, and therefore he is incapable of presenting any clear alternative.

Look at the past presidential campaign in the United States between Nixon, Wallace, and Humphrey. Nixon and Humphrey, because they try to consider themselves some sort of liberals, did not offer any alternatives. But Wallace did, he offered clear alternatives. Because Wallace was not afraid to alienate, he was not afraid to point out who had caused errors in the past, and who should be punished. The liberals are afraid to alienate anyone in society. They paint such a rosy picture of society and they tell us that while things have been bad in the past, somehow they can become good in the future without restructuring society at all.

What the liberal really wants is to bring about change which will not in any way endanger *his* position. The liberal says, "It is a fact that you are poor, and it is a fact that some people are rich; but we can make you rich without affecting those people who are rich." I do not know how poor people are going to get economic security without affecting the rich in a given country, unless one is going to exploit other peoples. I think that if we followed the logic of the liberal to its conclusion we would find that all we can get from it is that in order for a society to become equitable we must begin to exploit other peoples.

Fourth, I do not think that liberals understand the difference between influence and power, and the liberals get confused seeking influence rather than power. The conservatives on the right wing, or the fascists, understand power, though, and they move to consolidate power while the liberal pushes for influence.

Let us examine the period before civil rights legislation in the United States. There was a coalition of the labor movement, the student movement, and the church for the passage of certain civil rights legislation; while these groups formed a broad liberal coalition, and while they were able to exert their influence to get certain legislation passed, they did not have the power to implement the legislation once it became law. After they got certain legislation passed they had to ask the people whom they were fighting to implement the very things that they had not wanted to implement in the past. The liberal fights for influence to bring about change, not for the power to implement the change. If one really wants to change a society, one does not fight to influence change and then leave the change to someone else to bring about.

If the liberals are serious they must fight for power and not for influence.

These pitfalls are present in his politics because the liberal is part of the oppressor. He enjoys the status quo; while he himself may not be actively oppressing other people, he enjoys the fruits of that oppression. And he rhetorically tries to claim that he is disgusted with the system as it is.

While the liberal is part of the oppressor, he is the most powerless segment within that group. Therefore when he seeks to talk about change, he always confronts the oppressed rather than the oppressor. He does not seek to influence the oppressor, he seeks to influence the oppressed. He says to the oppressed, time and time again, "You don't need guns, you are moving too fast, you are too radical, you are too extreme." He never says to the oppressor, "You are too extreme in your treatment of the oppressed," because he is powerless among the oppressors, even if he is part of that group; but he has influence, or, at least, he is more powerful than the oppressed, and he enjoys this power by always cautioning, condemning, or certainly trying to direct and lead the movements of the oppressed.

To keep the oppressed from discovering his pitfalls the liberal talks about humanism. He talks about individual freedom, about individual relationships. One cannot talk about human idealism in a society that is run by fascists. If one wants a society that is in fact humanistic, one has to ensure that the political entity, the political state, is one that will allow humanism. And so if one really wants a state where human idealism is a reality, one has to be able to control the political state. What the liberal has to do is to fight for power, to go for the political state and then, once the liberal has done this, he will be able to ensure the type of human idealism in the society that he always talks about.

Because of the above reasons, because the liberal is

incapable of bringing about the human idealism which he preaches, what usually happens is that the oppressed whom he has been talking to finally becomes totally disgusted with the liberal and begins to think that the liberal has been sent to the oppressed to misdirect their struggle, to keep them confused so that the oppressor can continue to rule them. So whether the liberal likes it or not, he finds himself being lumped, by the oppressed, with the oppressor—of course he is part of that group. The final confrontation, when it does come about, will of course include the liberal on the side of the oppressor. Therefore if the oppressed really wants a revolutionary change, he has no choice but to rid himself of those liberals in his rank.

13

Message from Guinea

Brothers and sisters, I am very, very sorry that I cannot be with you for the opening of Malcolm X Liberation University—an event I consider one of the most important in our struggle. I say that it is important because of what this institution will mean to us, the direction that it should, must, and will give to our brothers and sisters who will be studying here. And it is a landmark—it marks the first time that we have got together among ourselves, sat down, and planned the ways and means by which our

Malcolm X Liberation University, October, 1969. (Delivered by Howard Fuller on behalf of Stokely Carmichael.)

young people in the United States will get a truly black education, an African education. This is also true for the Center of Black Education, which recently opened in Washington, D.C.; I understand it is a sister institution to Malcolm X Liberation University.

I have followed very closely the development of this institution through friends and co-workers who are helping to develop the school; they have sent over all the plans and information on the school, and I have taken all this information to Brother Sékou Touré, President of Guinea, and Brother Kwame Nkrumah, the legitimate President of Ghana. They, too, feel that this university represents one of the most fruitful and promising institutions inside the United States. And of course they fully support the underlying concepts that have guided and given direction to your efforts—the concept that we are all an African people, the concept that we are all working toward building a strong, united African nation wherever we may be, the concept that we must work toward the unification of Africa—in other words, the concept of Pan-Africanism.

When I look back over the past ten years of our struggle, from civil rights to Black Power, to where we are today, it becomes crystal clear to me that all of our efforts have gradually led us to where we as a people have to go, where we must go. Many of you who are present at the opening ceremonies of MXLU, and many of you who have helped develop this institution, spent many years working and organizing our people in the South—probably a good number have worked in SNCC. If we look back over those years, we remember that as we passed through all of these years we knew that what we were working on at that time was not the answer. But we had to work on programs such as sit-ins, freedom rides, freedom schools, freedom organizations, and community control just to develop political consciousness in our people and to heighten the contradictions in American society. We had to make our people see that America's interests are not our own best interest.

They never have been, they are not now, and they never will be.

In the early sixties, when we were fighting for the right to eat a hamburger next to white folks, most of us saw the sit-ins only as strategy and tactics to awaken the consciousness in our people—to get them to see what America was really about. Many of us went on to form "independent political organizations" and "freedom schools," and we knew that, again, this was only another step in heightening the contradictions in America. We had to convince our people that there is no place in the American political system for us. We then moved on to demands for Black Power, for community control of businesses, police, and schools, and so forth—but most of us recognized that this is not really possible in America, there is no way we can operate as an independent island surrounded by a hostile white community's police and military forces. All of these experiences and lessons have taught us that we must look only to *each other* in finding the solution of our problems—our solution cannot be found within America, even though those of us who live in the United States may remain there physically. We cannot look to our oppressors, those who oppress us, to liberate us or to even help in our liberation. For they will and must serve their own interest, which always involves oppressing us, the African peoples.

Now, we must recognize that black people, whether we are in Durham, San Francisco, Jamaica, Trinidad, Brazil, Europe or on the mother continent, are all an African people. We are Africans, there can be no question about that. We came from Africa, our race is African. The things that always distinguish us from white people, Europeans, are all African things. We have all suffered the same oppression at the hands of white folks, whether in Lynchburg, Virginia; Money, Mississippi; Accra, Ghana; or Johannesburg, South Africa, our oppression has been the same—we have all been colonized and dehumanized. It is also a question of our having common interests. It is in our best interest to wage an unrelenting struggle against Europe—and I include America as part of the European family—Americans, white folks, are Europeans. We must wage this struggle against the European world, since Europe and America must by definition keep us oppressed and brainwashed—if they are to survive. To keep herself alive and to support her racist, inhuman system, America must suck the lifeblood of Africa and African peoples, as she must also do in Asia and Latin America.

I would like to read some of Brother Malcolm's words. We must listen to Malcolm very closely, because we have to understand our heroes. We cannot let them be used by other people, we cannot let them be interpreted by other people to say other things. We must know and understand what our heroes were saying to us—*our* heroes, not the heroes of the white left or what have you.

Malcolm said,

> You cannot understand what is going on in Mississippi if you don't understand what is going on in the Congo, and you cannot really be interested in what's going on in Mississippi if you are not also interested in what's going on in the Congo. They're both the same. The same interests are at stake. The same ideas are drawn up. The same schemes are at work in the Congo that are at work in Mississippi. The same stake—no difference whatsoever.

And Brother Malcolm wrote a letter from Accra on May 11, 1964:

> Upon close study one can easily see a gigantic design to keep Africans here and the African-Americans from getting together. An African

178

official told me, "When one combines the number of people of African descent in South, Central and North America, they total well over 80,000,000. One can easily understand the attempts to keep the Africans from ever uniting with the African-Americans." Unity between Africans of the West and the Africans of the Fatherland will well change the course of history. Being in Ghana now, the fountainhead of Pan-Africanism, the last days of my tour should be intensely interesting and enlightening. Just as the American Jew is in harmony politically, economically, and culturally with world Jewry, it is time for all African-Americans to become an integral part of the world's Pan-Africanists, and even though we might remain in America physically while fighting for the benefits that the Constitution guarantees us, we must return to Africa philosophically and culturally, and develop a working unity in the framework of Pan-Africanism.

If we recognize and accept the truths Brother Malcolm was trying to tell us, it will be clear to us that to survive as a people we will go to war with America and Europe. Since they will do all in their power to protect their interest, this means they must oppress us and keep us in a semi-human state. We, in turn, will never be a strong, proud, free people unless we liberate Africa and take from America what America is trying to protect. Right now we are in a cold war with America and Europe. When we begin to move militarily on all fronts, it will be an all-out race war, Africa versus Europe. This may not seem pleasant to some of our brothers and sisters, but it is a question of who is going to survive—them or us. I think that the natural law of survival will answer that, even for those of us who recoil and do not want to face what is coming. I am reminded of what Brother Malcolm said in Chicago, way back in 1962: "What's good news for some is bad news for others."

For us to accomplish what we must accomplish and go where we must go, we are going to need skilled technicians with the political background to help us build a nation. When students come out of Malcolm X Liberation University, they will be in a position to offer their skills and services to our people wherever they are most needed, in America, Africa, the West Indies (which are really African islands, by the way), or Nova Scotia. Wherever you work, you will be contributing your efforts toward the building of a strong African nation.

The development of this institution is a living example of the development and growth of our struggle, because those of you who were the founders and gave direction to this school have all understood clearly what our struggle is all about. Through years of hard work, organizing, and learning, we have finally come full circle to recognizing the fact that we are an African people, that we must be about building a nation, that we must train and develop cadres of young brothers and sisters who will have the skills to help us do this.

The challenge that this presents to MXLU is overwhelming. Our people have waited four centuries for such people to come forth—all of our people have waited this long; some did not know that they were waiting for this, and some still do not know. Many are very slow in recognizing this fact, but they will eventually come around—the repression, oppression and depression of America will see to that.

You must never feel isolated or weak if you are attacked from outside our community or from within. The outside attacks will come from Europeans, white folks, who recognize that we have finally learned the truth about what we must do; they know that this spells their death and ushers in their funeral. The attacks from within will

180

come from our brothers and sisters who are where many of us were at some years ago. But they will come around. It is your job, it is our job, to bring them home. Here in Guinea, I am working very closely with Dr. Kwame Nkrumah. We are trying to aid the masses of Ghana who are striving to bring Nkrumah back to Ghana, to reinstall him as the legitimate President of Ghana, and to once again initiate a revolutionary Pan-Africanist government in that country—one that will serve as an English-speaking land base for our people in the Americas. The move must begin now and it is necessary that you give us all the support needed. In the past few years, we have seen America move against Ghana and Mali by overthrowing their governments; we have seen Brother Malcolm and Brother Patrice Lumumba assassinated by America; we have seen our revolutionary outposts dwindle down to almost nothing—all at the hands of the United States of America and her European sisters.

Guinea, one of the last remaining outposts of revolutionary African government in West Africa, is being isolated and harassed by America and Europe. There have been five attempted coups and assassination attempts against President Sékou Touré. Should such a coup ever prove successful, both Brothers Sékou Touré and Nkrumah would be wiped out—yes, wiped out. We cannot let this happen to two of our greatest leaders. They took Brother Malcolm and we did nothing. They took Patrice Lumumba and we did nothing. They took Pierre Mulele, also of the Congo, and we did nothing. We cannot sit back and allow them to off Brothers Sékou Touré and Nkrumah; we must move to give them protection and take some of the pressure off Guinea. One way we can begin to do this is to make sure that Dr. Nkrumah goes back to Ghana and reestablish another revolutionary base on the west coast of Africa. It is clear in my mind that this is a very necessary step toward the building of our nation, toward the total liberation of our people.

There is not too much more that I can say to you without going into a very lengthy discussion. Because of my work on this side of the ocean, in the motherland, I am not able to be with you today in Durham, at least not physically. I will be keeping in touch with your progress and development. As we as a people have always managed to do, we will find the ways to communicate, in spite of interference with mail, phone calls, and telegrams by "the man." In the near future I hope to have some pamphlets written so that we may go deeper into the discussion I have touched upon lightly today. It has indeed been an honor to greet you today, from Guinea. Don't ever think that Guinea or Africa is far away or that I have left you—we are much closer than you may think. We are moving ahead together, and we will work toward the day when we will once again walk the face of the earth as a proud, liberated, strong, and powerful people—not with just a few crumbs tossed out to us from America or control of meaningless institutions in our ghettos. We will be a unified people all over the world and on the continent. "Back to Africa" will not be just a dream, but it will be a reality. We will change the course of our history—we will get on the road to total liberation, and I am sure that Malcolm X Liberation University will become a driving force in our struggle.

With an undying love for black people wherever we may be,

Stokely

14

Pan-
Africanism

It's a great pleasure for me to be back in the United
States generally and in Atlanta in particular. It's good to
see such familiar faces, especially that of my lawyer, Mr.
Howard Moore, who has always stood close to me since
the very first time I met him, back in 1961, I believe. A
then young up-and-coming bourgeois lawyer, who gave
up financial success and became a true—and I think Chico
[Neblett] terms him correctly—black defender of the

Delivered at Morehouse College Gymnasium, Atlanta, Georgia,
April, 1970. Sponsored by the Institute of the Black World, with
excerpts from speech at Federal City College added to the body.
Washington, D.C., March, 1970.

movement because he always defends all of us anytime we call. And it is certainly good to have a man of the stature of Howard Moore inside our community who is always willing to come to our aid.

Many people said that when I left the United States fourteen months ago, I was running—that I was afraid. I want to deal with some of these attacks that have been thrown my way during the past months. I don't want to attack any personalities because I have never done that, and I learned that from Dr. Martin Luther King. I've never attacked any black man even though I've been attacked by almost all of them—the ones on the right and the ones who are supposed to be revolutionary. Dr. King never attacked any black man and that's why I had a great deal of respect and admiration for him—because he cared about his people and he always sought to unify us rather than to divide us. But I must speak to some of the criticisms because I think it's necessary for us to clear up our minds. A lot of the criticisms have not been on a political level, but on a personal level; that means my critics are incapable of dealing with my political ideology and must therefore attack me personally. That shows the very weakness of their political position. Stokely Carmichael isn't Stokely Carmichael because he's Stokely Carmichael. He's Stokely Carmichael because of the political ideology he expresses and that's why people listen to him and pay any attention to him. So if you are attacking Stokely Carmichael, you must attack the political ideology that he expresses, not Stokely Carmichael the person. When you begin to attack the person, you admit you are incapable of attacking his political ideology.

What have been the attacks? The people who said I was afraid, unfortunately, were people who just became revolutionary last week or last year. Many of those now calling me afraid overlook the fact that when I was in Mississippi, as a young man of nineteen, facing guns and bullets, some of them were raping black women and writing love letters to white girls—very revolutionary acts, no doubt.

When Willie Ricks [former SNCC organizer and field secretary] and I were calling for Black Power in Mississippi in 1966, they didn't even know they were black. In this very city, Atlanta, Georgia (where I understand I have also come under some heavy attacks because I am supposed to be afraid), I was the first black man to be arrested by Mayor Ivan Allen for inciting to riot. My defender then was again my attorney, Mr. Moore. At that time, most people were afraid of the concept Black Power. Obviously, these people who say I'm afraid do not understand revolution. They think revolution is about yelling and screaming. They actually believe that they can get up on T.V. and rap their way out of the trouble we find ourselves in. They do not recognize that if one is truly a revolutionary, one must understand that one must take time out to study.

Because revolutionary theories are based on historical analyses, one must study. One must understand one's history and one must make the correct historical analysis. At the correct moment you make your historical leap and carry the struggle forward. Not only that, you cannot rap if you really don't believe what you're saying, or if you don't know the answers. Fourteen months ago it became clear to me that the black community was heading for political chaos. I knew that I didn't have the answers, so it was silly for me to stay here and keep rapping about what I didn't know. Why should I stay here to get up on television and yell a lot of nonsense? It would only cause confusion in my community. I don't want to do that. Confusion is the greatest enemy of revolution.

If you're talking twenty-four hours a day to rallies, to television, to the press, you don't have time to read the newspapers, let alone read your history. You can't be revolutionary off the top of your head. How can you do that, you're jiving with your people. Jiving with them. I thought the best thing I could do if I really cared about the interests of my people was to go somewhere to study and try and understand more clearly the forces of history. Therefore, at the invitation of the president of Guinea, Mr. Ahmed Sékou Touré, I went to study under the man I consider the most brilliant in the world today—Osagyefo, Dr. Kwame Nkrumah.

Many people have also attacked me for my funds. They said, "Carmichael doesn't work, how come he's running here and running there?" If anybody knows anything about lectures series, they will know that the people who invite you always supply the funds for your transport. So whenever I'm invited to speak, the host supplies the funds for that transportation.

I also fell under attack by organizations that I'd helped to build. For example: I worked with the Student Nonviolent Coordinating Committee since its very inception. I helped build that organization, I gave it my skills. That organization fired me. I was expelled from the organization because I was supposed to have had a $70,000 house. No one took the time out to check whether or not their brother who had worked with them had the $70,000 house. They just accepted the word of the white man, and they were supposed to be political. So they expelled me for having a $70,000 house. I am still waiting for my house. But I didn't waste time answering these accusations because they were not engaged in a personal battle with Stokely Carmichael but a political one. I represented a political ideology, whether I had a $7,000 house, a $70,000 house or a $270,000 house. That was not the issue. The issue was the political ideology of Stokely Carmichael. I want to keep stressing this because in the years ahead of us there will be more attacks on the personalities, and we must not be bogged down with those attacks. We must always ask what is the attack on his political ideology. SNCC attacked me, but I never attacked them. I will never attack any black man. That is causing divisions inside our community, and if they cared about our community, they would try to bring about unity instead of division. *At this period of our struggle, unity is paramount.*

In 1965 I organized the first Black Panther Party in this country in Lowndes County, Alabama. It was a party organized around a political platform of black independent politics with guns. When I went to California in 1966, Huey P. Newton and Bobby Seale came to me and asked me if they could organize a Black Panther Party in the Bay area. I agreed to that. I left the country and went traveling around. When I came back to the country Huey P. Newton had been shot and jailed. I had heard about it when I was in Tanzania. We had a rally in Tanzania for Huey, because I had always been impressed with the Minister of Defense of the Black Panther Party and always had a great deal of respect for him. When he was in jail, Eldridge Cleaver and Bobby Seale came to me and asked me would I help them get some publicity for Huey because they said to me that no other black man in the country would help. I said, of course—there ain't no doubt about it. I explained to them that we had different political ideologies and were going in different directions but because of my love for Huey P. Newton I would work with them. We got out of the bind by saying that I would become Honorary Prime Minister, which means I would speak for the Party, but I would have nothing to do with the functioning of the Party. I accepted this. I was concerned about Huey P. Newton. I felt that we needed all of the noble warriors that we could have out here educating the masses of our people rather than sitting in jail. The Panthers and I, of course, began to go in different ways in our political philosophy. I came back to Washington, D.C., and I organized the Black United Front. The Panthers went in a different direction. The contradictions began to mount more and more and, finally, I felt we had to part forces. I merely wrote a letter resigning from the Black Panther Party. I never attacked them. Yet before and after my resignation they attacked me every time they got a chance. That is their wish. They may do that as long as they like.

I will never attack the Black Panther Party. I will attack political concepts that I think are damaging our people, and when I do that I will give my affirmative political concept. In our community today we have people who have no program other than attacking other people's programs. That's not the way you build revolution. We have many organizations in our community. We have the New Republic of Africa. We have the Muslims. We have the NAACP. We have the Urban League. We have SCLC. We have the Panthers. These organizations should come before the masses and affirmatively state what their program is, then let the masses decide which political philosophy they want to follow, that is, if one is truly concerned about organizing his people. At least that's my feeling. I tell you this history because I think it is important for you to know and to understand it. What I have given you is the truth. It is even documented in Eldridge Cleaver's book *Post-Prison Writings and Speeches,* so you should read that yourself and get that documentation.

Many people said I was a coward. They said I ran. When I came back, they said I was a CIA agent. Can't win for losing. Many said that I was in "self-imposed exile." Obviously that is incoherent nonsense. How could I be in exile when I am at home in Africa, where I came from, and when I left of my own free will?

All revolutions are based on historical analysis. Karl Marx bases his scientific study of the economic forces in an industrialized society on historical materialism. He says, and he is correct, that one must understand historical materialist forces in the society, and that means a complete study of those forces and a correct analysis. Malcolm X, in *Malcolm X Speaks,* in the essay "Message to the Grassroots," says that of all the studies, history rewards us best. So Brother Malcolm X recognized the necessity of history.

I speak before the Institute of the Black World, a forum that is trying to combine all of the studies of the black world and, according to it, make its focal point the writings and the research of the late Dr. Martin Luther King, Jr. I think most of us would agree with that. We may have some quibble about whether or not Dr. King's works should be the focal point of the Institute of the Black World, but none of us would quibble about the fact that his works must certainly be included because he contributed a fantastic amount of knowledge, time and energy to our movement. What we must not allow, just because he becomes the focal point, is a misinterpretation of history. I saw, for example, the Dr. Martin Luther King film a few weeks ago as soon as I entered the country, and I was very amazed to see that they left out the entire Black Power march in Mississippi! I don't know who the people are who made the film, but I need to tell them that they cannot mess with the forces of history. They may try to say what they want, but the fact is that the Black Power march in Mississippi was an important factor in the lives of black people in this country and to leave that out is to try to mess with the forces of history. If you try to mess with the forces of history, you get crushed by the forces of history. So this is a fact. We cannot allow them to paint Dr. King into what he was not.

Martin Luther King taught us many things. We must understand what he taught us and accept it. He taught us how to confront. Dr. King did—not the Black Panther Party, not Malcolm X—Dr. Martin Luther King did. His tactic was nonviolence but he did teach us how to confront, and confront he did. We thank him for that. And he taught us how to mobilize the masses.

Dr. King, however, was not an astute politician, he was a man of the pulpit. For example, Dr. King never took a political position against the war in Vietnam, he always took a moral position against the war. There is nothing wrong with that. As a minister, he has the right to do that. But most of us have always taken political positions against the war in Vietnam. Dr. King was not the first black man to come out against the war in Vietnam in this country, nor was SCLC the first organization. The Student Nonviolent Coordinating Committee was the first organization on a nationwide basis to do that. It is important for us to document our history and to document it correctly because, again, it is from our history that we make our analysis and understand revolutionary processes.

There are stages of liberation movement. The first stage is waking up our people. We have to wake them up to the impending danger. So we yell, Gun! Shoot! Burn! Kill! Destroy! They're committing genocide! until the masses of our people are awake. Once they are awake, it is the job of the revolutionary intelligentsia to give them the correct political ideology. We don't have it in this country—what we have in this country is an attitude, not an ideology; the attitude, the idea of confrontation, was started in our generation by Dr. King. And he was the first. You shouldn't knock him for preaching nonviolence. The historical conditions only permitted nonviolent demonstrations at the time Dr. King started; nonviolence was the only possibility. All of you who condemn Dr. King today, you didn't start talking about armed struggle until 1966, '67, '68, '69 or last week. How could Dr. King talk about violence?

When I was a student at Howard University we almost got thrown out of school for bringing Malcolm X to speak there because we thought he had something to say. Malcolm X could not speak at many black institutions. When he spoke he was attacked by everybody, he was called crazy, irresponsible, stupid, this, that, and the minds of black people in this country were so whitewashed that they believed it. This is history. If the minds of people had been alert when Brother Malcolm X was offed, the same thing would have happened then that happened after Dr. Martin Luther King was offed. You should see the development of historical conditions. Dr. King preached nonviolence, Malcolm X said Yeah, we need guns to protect ourselves. Malcolm X got offed; we did nothing. Dr. King got offed; we tore up the country. It's a historical development of the people. The people. Dr. King worked with what he had, and he gave us confrontation. We took that confrontation and we worked with it, and we worked with it and we developed it into armed struggle or at least to the point where we can talk about armed struggle.

Now then, this whole black world from South Africa to Nova Scotia is in political chaos merely because it has no ideology. If one does not have an ideology one can have no discipline. That's been the problem of the black community. The Muslims, for example, have discipline. They have discipline because they have the same ideology. In the Christian Church, you have discipline. You have a structure. In order for the black community to come together we must find a common ideology. It is in seeking to find this common ideology that I come before you tonight. An ideology is merely a cohesive force, a set of principles, a set of beliefs that tell us where we're going, what our goals are, and what we hope to achieve. Underneath that will come the tactics that give us the best way to achieve these goals. If I said that all of us decided that we wanted to go from here to downtown Atlanta, that would be our ideology—that's our goal. We may argue about how best to get there, but we have the ideology—where we want to go. We want to go to downtown Atlanta. The problem in the black community today is that there are always arguments over tactics because there is no ideology. So you have people who are arguing about how to go, but they don't know where they are going. That's why we find so much confusion among black student unions and black college campus groups. They are arguing about tactics. They are arguing about how to go, but they haven't

191

decided where they want to go. Before you decide where you want to go, before you find your ideology, you must analyze what your problems are.

The black community today faces two problems: capitalism and racism. Some people in our community say that if you eliminate capitalism, you will automatically eliminate racism. I say this is not true. While I agree that capitalism reinforces racism and racism reinforces capitalism, it is nonsensical to say that if we got rid of capitalism we would automatically get rid of racism. There are many so-called communist and socialist societies in the world today that are rampant with racism. I don't argue about which came first, whether capitalism produced racism or vice versa, but I say that racism today, even if it *were* produced by capitalism, has taken on such proportions, such institutions, that it has become an entity unto itself, and it must be dealt with as a separate entity.

In discussing capitalism and racism, I want to give a Marxist analysis of this society. I want to say that I'm not a Marxist-Leninist myself but I understand Karl Marx better than many people who call themselves Marxists-Leninists. He did not deal with the question of race; and in the twentieth century we see that race has not only become a phenomenon with the proportions of a class structure, but in many cases it has itself become an entity and a class unto itself. Let me explain that. Many people in this country are running around talking about black capitalism and black capitalists. Those people who are doing that do not understand capitalism. Karl Marx defines capitalist. He says that a capitalist is someone who owns and controls the means of production. He is absolutely correct. There is no other definition for a capitalist. There are people who work for the capitalist called the bourgeoisie. These are people who serve the interests of capitalism. Lenin calls them the lackeys of capitalism. Mao Tse-tung calls them "running dogs of capitalism."

There are potential capitalists, there are aspiring capitalists, but the only capitalist is someone who actually owns and controls the means of production. If you understand this definition according to Marx, then you will know that there is no such thing as a black capitalist anywhere in the world today.

Now, if we understand that, we can clear up a lot of the misunderstanding that has been disseminated in our community. One must always study. Marx says that the capitalists are death, that there is no hope for the capitalist. According to Marx, they must be killed. He says their underlying motive is profit. They will do anything for profit, so you can never stop them or get any concessions from them; they must be killed. If you understand that, then you know that all the capitalists in the world today are white. According to Karl Marx—not according to Stokely Carmichael, but according to Karl Marx.

Below the capitalist you have the bourgeoisie. These are the people who serve the interests of capitalism. For example, the owners of corporations are capitalists. The man who owns and controls General Motors is a capitalist. But the managerial director is not a capitalist. He is a lackey of capitalism. He's a member of the bourgeoisie. We have white lackeys of capitalism, and we have the black lackeys of capitalism, yet these two groups are incapable of coming together because of the question of race. These are not the misdirected masses. The capitalists need to have these two groups come together because, according to Marx, the natural ally of the capitalist is the bourgeoisie. It is in the interest of the capitalist to have the white lackeys and the black lackeys come together because they are the ones who are going to fight for him. Yet the capitalists in this country are incapable of bringing them together, again because of the question of race. Because, according to Karl Marx, the white lackeys of capitalism and the black lackeys of capitalism should come together because it is the class interest that binds these people together, and since they have the same class interest, they should come together, but they do not because of race.

On the bottom of Marx's analysis, of course, you have the urban proletariat, the workers, the peasants, the factory workers, the landless, misdirected masses. According to Marx these are the people who will lead the inevitable class struggle. We have seen that poor whites and poor blacks are incapable of coming together in this country, or when they do come together, we see it is the white man who benefits and having gained what he wants he turns against the black man. We have seen that time and time again. All coalitions of the two groups have always worked to the disadvantage of the black man. Let us view all coalitions between white groups and black groups in this country historically. There have been a number of them. We can go back to the Populist movement in Georgia and Tom Watson immediately after the Civil War. You remember the Populist movement? Tom Watson—came to black people, asked them to join hands with him to fight the white capitalists who were fleecing both of them. The black man joined with him, and after Mr. Watson secured political power, he turned on the black man, and advocated lynching. That's history. We must remember that all revolutions are based on history. We must remember Brother Malcolm telling us that we must study history.

We can come up a little further and document the history of the labor movement in this country in the 1930s. The white workers came into the black community once again asking us to join with them and wage battle and we did that and today we cannot even get into the labor unions in this country. I know you are aware of these movements because you have read *Black Power* by Carmichael and Hamilton.

Recently, we had the coalition of the Black Panther Party and the Peace and Freedom Party. It should be analyzed in two areas—class and race. Marx says that the bourgeoisie will always come together and fight for the interests of the capitalist. But he says there are individuals inside the bourgeoisie who will betray their class interests and join the masses and fight with the masses. We have clear examples of that. Fidel Castro was a member of the aristocracy in Cuba. He betrayed his class interests, joined the masses, and led a successful revolution. Mao Tse-tung was an up-and-coming college student in China. He betrayed his class interests and led a successful revolution. So Marx says that there are individuals in this class who will betray their class interest and join us and fight. But Marx says we cannot expect all of them to join us because as a class they represent the economic interests of the capitalists. They're the lackeys of capitalism. We see the Black Panther Party, which is supposed to represent the lumpen proletariat, the class that is economically insecure. They form an alliance with the Peace and Freedom Party, which represents the bourgeoisie, the economically secure. It is totally un-Marxist for the economically secure to make a coalition with the economically insecure, because the economically secure are not going to fight. "Workers of the world unite, you have nothing to lose but your chains." This is precisely what Marx was talking about: only those who have nothing to lose will fight. That has been proven if you analyze the situation in a racial context also. The Peace and Freedom Party made the alliance with the Black Panther Party. Today, we see twenty-eight members of the Black Panther Party dead. There is not one dead member of the Peace and Freedom Party—not one! We see the Chicago Seven after their fiasco in Chicago allowed to smoke pot on T.V. and go scot free, yet Bobby Seale is sitting up in jail. A clear analysis will once again show us that whenever these coalitions are made it is the black man who comes out at the bottom of the ladder.

Many people are carried away today thinking that the

hippies and the yippies and the white mother-country radicals are revolutionary. They are not. What they engaged in at Chicago was what Lenin called "infantile disorder." And that is precisely what it is. This country, we all agree, is moving toward fascism. When a country moves towards fascism, the most important right of the people is the right to demonstrate. The people in Chicago were arrested because of the right to demonstrate. But rather than continue to argue their case on their right to demonstrate, they concentrated on some nonsensical wearing of robes, cussing out a judge, laughing, and all of this nonsense, theatrics, and theater of the absurd. Nobody talks about the right to demonstrate; they talk about the courts. And what happened? They have given the courts an excuse to become more fascist. From their antics came three decisions from the courts: one, a defendant may be gagged and bound; two, he may be kept in prison until he agrees to be quiet; and third, they can conduct trials on closed circuit T.V., and now the Panther 21 must face the results of this fascist decision. Therefore, before we talk about alliances we must build our power base so that we are strong enough to achieve the gains we want and we depend upon no one but ourselves. The first law of revolution is "the law of self-sufficiency."

Some people see the fight on our hands and they get so scared they start going to white folks for allies. They say, "We need allies, we can't do it ourselves." They're not revolutionary. Because a revolutionary is self-sufficient! He depends upon himself first, foremost, and last. If he gets aid from a friendly country, he can accept it, but if he's dependent upon that country for aid then he accepts the ideology and/or advice of the nation that gave him aid.

Today we need a clear understanding of where we're going. It is no longer necessary for brothers to scream about guns and what we are going to do. To be revolutionary one must pick up the gun, but merely picking up the gun does not make you revolutionary. And we must understand this very carefully. There are a lot of brothers with guns. Some are shooting us! That's not revolutionary! Merely because one has a gun in his hands does not make one revolutionary. What makes one revolutionary is not only having the gun, but the political ideology to go along with the gun. And that political ideology must speak the needs and aspirations of the masses of our people. Once you have that, plus the gun, then you have a revolutionary, because revolutionaries always fight on two levels: the political and the military.

I want to go back to Malcolm X for a minute. In the same "Message to the Grassroots," Brother Malcolm says, in the final analysis all revolutions are fought over the question of land. He gives the example of the Chinese revolution and he gives the example of the Algerian revolution. He gives the example of the Mau Mau movement in Kenya. And over and over again, throughout the "Message," Brother Malcolm keeps saying that in the final analysis revolution is fought over the question of land. Brother Malcolm is not the only one who says this. Mao Tse-tung says this. Ho Chi Minh says this. Fidel Castro says this. V. I. Lenin says this. Osagyefo says this. And Stokely Carmichael, as humble as I am, also says this.

Eldridge Cleaver quotes from Marx in his latest pamphlet, *Revolution and Education*. He says that if we're fighting we must control the land because it is upon the land that we build the superstructure. Superstructure is a Marxist term, but I know that all of you have dealt at least with Marx and so you know what superstructure is. You read the Panther paper. They mention the word all the time. The superstructure is merely the intertwining, interlocked type of system that you have—the political, economic, and social system. But the superstructure is always based on the land. Revolution must be about land. It is from the land that we get everything we need for survival. It is from the land that we get our clothes, in the form of cotton. It is from the land that we get our food and the animals we take meat from. It is from the land that we get the mineral resources necessary for the development of a technological society. So we see that if we're talking about revolution, and if we're talking very seriously about revolution, we must be talking about land. Brother Malcolm is absolutely correct, many people say that they follow Brother Malcolm X. Unfortunately a lot of them do not read Brother Malcolm X. They just quote or misquote him. But it is time for us now to take time out to sit down and study and understand the things that Brother Malcolm X was talking about.

Mao Tse-tung says politics is war without bloodshed. War is politics with bloodshed. Remember what Malcolm X says—"in the final analysis, all revolution is fought over the question of land." If we understand that, then we recognize the need for a land base. We see now that we have the three necessary ingredients if we're to talk about ideology—we must speak to the problem of class, against capitalism; we must speak to the problem of race, against racism; and we must speak to the problem of land.

If we go back to our history, we will note that the groups that have the largest success in our community are those groups that deal with the question of land, class, and race. The Honorable Marcus Garvey organized around the concept of land in 1922—Back to Africa. Marcus Garvey had the largest organization in this country among black people. No other organization past or present has been able to match Mr. Garvey, simply because he dealt with the question of land, the question of race, and the question of class. If you knew Brother Malcolm X you would know that his basic ideology is Garveyism. His father was a Garveyite. Always we must understand our history, because we will see how it moves—from Garvey to Malcolm's father, on to Malcolm, on down the line. The second largest organization that we've had, the largest one in our community, is the Muslims, again, because they are attempting to deal with the question of land, race, and class. Any organization that calls itself a revolutionary organization must deal with the question of land. I want to talk about European settler colonies because, again, we're dealing with land. A settler colony is an area of land where the European leaves Europe, comes to that area and takes over the land, and dominates the traditional owners of the land. My wife is from South Africa. South Africa is a settler colony. Rhodesia, which is really named Zimbabwe, is a settler colony. Europeans changed the name of Zimbabwe to Rhodesia, changed the name so that it appears as if they have always belonged there. Because if they say they're Rhodesians and they come from Rhodesia you never question it and it appears as if they are the traditional owners of that land. You must understand the trick. The settlers' aim is to make the colony an extension of their original country. Mozambique is a settler colony. Angola is a settler colony. Portuguese Guinea is a settler colony. Australia is a settler colony. My brothers and sisters, Israel is a settler colony. European Jews leave Europe, go to Palestine, change the name to Israel, expel the original inhabitants, the Palestinian Arabs, and dominate the land.

But, my brothers and sisters, more importantly for you and for me, we must come to understand that America and Canada are settler colonies. You have been white-washed into believing that there was such a thing called the American Revolution. There was never such an animal. It was just sons fighting their parents for who's going to take the loot. George Washington was born in England. He was fighting to control this piece of land. He wasn't fighting a revolutionary fight. Revolution overturns systems, destroys, it's bloody, it knows no compromise. What system did they overturn? None. They had slaves and they were taking this land from the red man. What system? They did the same thing in what they call

Rhodesia, when they broke from England, in November 1965. The only difference is that the Rhodesians couldn't afford armed struggle today because the political consciousness of the masses is aroused. But they could afford it in 1776, and then had the nerve to talk about the glorious American Revolution! What revolution? They were colonialists, they were not colonies. They were part of the mother country. Yes, they were white radicals from the mother country, England. America and Canada are settler colonies, but it is difficult for us to understand that because they are close to being successful settler colonies. *In order to be a successful settler colony, one must commit genocide against the traditional owners of the land.* That is exactly what the Europeans have done. After committing genocide, they changed the name to America. When you call them Americans, you make it sound as if they belong here. You do that because you want to call yourselves black Americans and you want to feel that you belong here too. But if we analyze history and if we agree that revolutions are based on historical analysis, we will see that they are not Americans, they are in fact European settlers. That's all they are. Now I know what you will say: "Oh, but that happened a long time ago." It might have happened five thousand years ago. I'm talking about history and fact. It is a fact that they are European settlers. And our ideology *must* analyze history.

If they are European settlers, guess what we are? We can't be Afro-Europeans or black Europeans. We have to be an African people. See, if we say we are Americans, black Americans, or Afro-Americans, it means that we participated in committing genocide against the red man, and support the genocide that "Americans" are committing in Vietnam, Asia, Africa, and Latin America. Since we did not, there's no need for us to call ourselves black Americans. There is something you must understand about this problem of "Afro-American" and "black American." You can be walking down the street and you may see a person who is of Chinese descent. They look Chinese, right? Now they may have been in America for as many generations as we have been here. They may not be able to speak a word of Chinese, but when you see them, the first thing you say is "That's a Chinaman." You never say that's a Chino-American, because there are two levels on which one is identified. One is identified by one's nationality—that's what your passport is, the papers you carry—and by one's ancestral bearing. Yet for all other people, as soon as we recognize them on the street we never question their nationality. We always go back to their ancestral bearings. They're Chinese or Japanese, or they're Indians—except us. When it comes to us, the first question is, Where are you from? "Oh, I'm from Jamaica." "Oh, you're a West Indian." "Where are you from?" "I'm from Georgia." "Oh, you're an American." "Where're you from?" "I'm from Kenya." "Oh, you're a Kenyan." "Where're you from?" "I'm from Ghana." "Oh, you're a Ghanaian." No, my brothers and sisters, we are all Africans.

This concept must become clear in our minds, especially since we say we're dealing with the question of capitalism and racism. Everyone knows that the racist of the world is that European white boy. There's no need to even discuss that. A settler colony is, by its very nature, an unjust and immoral political state. Wherever the European has gone, he has set up a settler colony, whether he is the majority or the minority. There are Europeans in Palestine, in South Africa, in Mozambique, in Australia, in Canada, in the United States, in Latin America—wherever he has gone he has established settler colonies. He has a settler complex.

I have outlined what I think have been some of the problems and some of the areas in which we must move that logically lead to Pan-Africanism. Many people have accepted the slogan of Black Power, some people have tried to make it mean what they want it to mean. The highest political expression of Black Power is Pan-Africanism. Black Power means that all people who are black should come together, organize themselves and form a power base to fight for their liberation. That's Black Power.

Unfortunately, my adopted tribe in America is very tribalistic. They think that Black Power means only them. They actually think they are the only black people in the world. Obviously, we must tell our brothers and sisters in America that this just isn't so. There are black people in South America, there are black people in the Caribbean and there are a whole lot of black people in Africa. Black Power must mean all of these peoples. It has to, unless you want to be a racist and discriminate against other black people.

It must be Pan-Africanism, because we said that in a revolution one must have a land base. Now we must discuss where black people in this country can best get a land base. This is where the difficulty will arise. Many people will say that we can get a land base in America. If we're fighting against capitalism inside America, and if we know anything about capitalism, we know that the white boy isn't going to give up any land. You must take every inch of the ground from him. The revolutionary formula for taking land is simply seize, hold, develop, and expand. That's how we're going to have to take land in this country. We'll have to seize it, we'll have to hold it, and we'll have to develop it. We see clearly from the Muslims' example that even when they try to buy the land, the white boy won't let them have it. If we could seize the land we wouldn't be able to hold it, and if we could hold it, we wouldn't be able to develop it.

Many people say in this country that we should take Louisiana, Mississippi, Georgia, South Carolina, and North Carolina and make those our United States. Now let's examine those states. Louisiana gives us some oil. Birmingham has some steel. The vast areas of these states are agricultural states. They produce cotton and tobacco. So that means that if we took these states and set up a nation we would have the greatest cotton- and tobacco-growing nation in the world. However, we wouldn't have any industry because there are no mineral resources to be found in these states. And if we're fighting against imperialism, we realize that our enemy is a highly technological enemy, so we must develop technology in order to fight him. If we seized this land, if we held this land, we would have an agricultural society. From what would we produce our tanks, airplanes, and guns—those things that are necessary to fight imperialism? An agricultural nation could never defeat an industrial society. Therefore, we must ask ourselves where best can we get land. My brothers and sisters, I ask you to look with me to Africa.

It is the richest continent in the world. It has all of the mineral resources necessary for the highest technological society in the world today. It has bauxite, copper, zinc, diamonds, gold, oil, ore, cocoa. Man it's even got peanuts, that's how rich it is.

It seems to me any clear black ideology that talks about revolution, understanding the necessity of a land base, must be pointed toward Africa, especially since we've decided that we're an African people and Africa belongs to all African peoples. It is our homeland! Those people who don't look toward Africa consider themselves Americans. That's their right. They want to consider themselves Americans, they have the right to fight for this land, take it from the white boy, exterminate the red man and then keep it. For me, I don't want to be a part of that. We must ask ourselves what relationship Africa has to us while we are here in the Western Hemisphere. We must ask what our relationship to Africa is and how do we survive here at the same time. Having answered those two questions, we have found the key to our ideology. We know that we came from Africa. We may not want to call ourselves Africans, but we cannot deny that we were stolen from Africa.

Let's examine power and how it protects the individual. When a white boy comes into our community, we are not afraid of that white boy as an individual; we are afraid of him because of the power he represents. And he is respected wherever he goes. When we see an African anywhere in the world he is not respected because there is no power behind him. That is precisely why the European can go all over the world and people bow down to him— because of the power he represents. Where are we going to get power from? The hippies? Is that being revolutionary? By cursing? Is that the best they can teach us? They tell me that Malcolm X came from the grass roots, they told me he came from the gutter, from the slums, they told me he was in jail. I have heard him speak many times and I have never heard him curse. Never. Because he respected his people. Revolution is not about being dirty or about cursing but about giving our people the finer things in life. If we want to curse or shoot dope, cut each other or stand still, then we don't have to fight. You know, we can stay right here and do it. We are fighting to get out of those conditions, not to stay in them. Nobody risks his life to shoot dope, or risks his life to curse, or risks his life to prove how bad he is—we are fighting other people to get rid of oppression, we want a better way of life. That's why we fight.

You saw that white boy Dick Cavett—when I was on his show, he wanted to talk about the shades and about the college, he didn't want to talk about what we were supposed to talk about. You can run but you can't hide, you've got to come to it sometime or later. But they're not going to let us on their T.V. show and really break down the truth to our people. The only people they're going to let on T.V. are those going through the streets yelling

"Yeah, we're going to kill you, we're going to do this or that, which only gives the honky an excuse to move farther into fascism and prepare to wipe us out. These are the ones who are not giving us the political ideology. We need political ideology. We are divided fighting ourselves merely because we don't know where we're going or what we want. Some say all we want is freedom, we just want freedom. Some say we want peace, everybody wants peace. I don't want peace. I want power.

The African has no power anywhere!

The same question that the Honorable Marcus Garvey asked in 1922 is still relevant today: Where is the black man's government? Where is the government that is going to speak for our protection? If Mother Africa was unified, my brothers and sisters, as quiet as it's kept, it would be the most powerful continent in the world. More powerful than this monster, more powerful than China, more powerful than Russia. It would be the most powerful continent in the world. It could then give protection to all its descendants, wherever they may be.

We're dealing with the relationship of power, and I say we must make Africa our priority. We must deal clearly now with Africa and begin to support the movements for liberation on the continent. If you have children, you give your children everything, because they represent the future. Your mothers and fathers worked very hard for you to come to college because you represent the future. If we are honest with ourselves, we know that there is no future in Babylon, U.S.A.

We see the black bourgeoisie having many problems because there is no viable alternative for them to earn a living. They must give their skills to the white boy, and they're becoming more worried with the fact that this is the only way for them to make a living. There is no possible way for them to build a nation within this country. It is possible for our people to begin to build a nation inside Mother Africa. A true revolutionary must provide a viable alternative, not just rhetoric condemning the existing system.

The Jews set the precedent. European Jews, who live here and function inside this American political system, get up and talk about Israel. Whenever Jewish senators take the floor they wage propaganda for Israel. As a matter of fact, when the President of France came here, European Jews, 4,000 strong, picketed him because he was giving fighter planes to Libya, which is in Africa! My brothers and sisters, do you not recognize what these European Jews were saying? They were saying that Africa has no right to have any guns, but Israel has the right to have all the guns she wants. Do you know that right now the so-called state of Israel is fighting Egypt? Are you not aware of the fact that Egypt is part of Africa? So you have European Jews, who are talking about Israel, occupying land in Palestine that doesn't belong to them, supporting that concept—and here we are, from Africa, we belong to that land, and we are not supporting it!

What should we do? Should we all go back to Africa? "Are you saying we should all go back to Africa?" No, I am not saying we should all go back to Africa at this point. We all have to go back there sooner or later though. If this white boy keeps on going the way he's going, a whole lot of people will be running as fast as they can go to get there. No, we're not saying that. What we're saying is that we must begin to understand Africa, not only culturally, but politically, and we must begin to support those movements of liberation that seek to build truly revolutionary states in Africa that will support us. In the meantime, in our own communities, we should do three things. Number one, we should seek to unify our community. We're not blind; we see genocide around the corner. Political groups who have disagreements should try and keep their disagreements under the table, rather than attacking each other, calling names like "pork chop nationalists" and "cultural nationalists," or "CIA agents" and playing into the hands of our enemies. Keep that in the background. Don't attack anybody, just say what you've got to say, brother. Run your program to the people and let them decide. If you believe you have the correct ideology, all you have to do is get before the masses of your people, state your ideology and go to work. If they agree with you, they'll come with you; if they don't agree with you, they'll go with the other person. If they go with the other person, you're wrong. Whether you admit it or not you're wrong because in a revolution it is the masses who decide, not the self-appointed vanguard. We must seek to unify our community.

Second, we must seek to take over all of the political institutions inside our community: the police station, the judicial system, the board of education, the welfare system, especially the education system, because education is nothing but an ideology, you're hip to that. Ninety per cent of your education is the ideology of that society. We need to give our people the correct political ideology; therefore, we've got to have these schools. But we know that today we are not going to have these schools without confrontation. Overt, open confrontation, however, is no longer the way. We're going to organize politically to take them over. If we don't get them, there will be political consequences against those people who are standing in the path of the masses—again because of history.

All of the political institutions inside our community should be taken over, and they can be taken over today without confrontation. The stage we have reached is that of education, not confrontation! In an army you don't just keep confronting, confronting, confronting, like cowboys and Indians riding from New York to California. You don't do that. In a revolution, you confront, you seize, you hold, you develop—then, after you're ready, you go again. You seize, you hold, you develop, you expand, you stop, you go again. If you keep confronting, confronting,

confronting, and you don't organize what you have gained, you leave your rear open for attack by the enemy. And that's precisely what's happening in the black community today and on many black college campuses today. We refuse to take time out to organize our people—the real work in revolution.

America is showing the internal contradictions of capitalism Marx speaks about. She is obviously divided. Now, what we know about white folks is that they're always united around one question—*us*. On the question of race, white America is a monolithic structure. Therefore, since the country must move to fascism in order to avoid internal collapse, we must not allow the white leaders of this country to use us for the justification of that fascism. We must allow them to have their internal contradictions, justify it among themselves while we quietly organize and educate our masses so that when they come we will be well prepared to meet them. We're not prepared to meet them now! They're also not completely prepared to meet us now. That means that time must be put to the best use. We must begin to organize and prepare for the inevitable confrontation.

Thirdly, we must try to develop independent economic bases beginning with our organizations. When our organizations become economically independent, they will speak to our needs. Now that responsibility is on all of us. Merely clapping is not going to do it. That means it must be our responsibility to donate money to those organizations—to be willing to pay dues. We've been talking about "they getting support from the white man," but that's because nobody's been supporting them. Now *we* must begin to support them, because then we can hire and fire them. Yes sir, praise the Lord, we need to do that. Once again, we must caution that these economic bases cannot make money for individuals but must be used to benefit the entire black community. We must understand that most, if not all, of these enterprises in our community are incapable of producing goods, because we do not own or control the means of production in the larger society. But we must nonetheless attempt to establish independent economic bases wherever possible.

Now, many say that I am counterrevolutionary because I am speaking out against drugs in the community. Unfortunately, they know nothing about the history of revolution. If they did they would know that Mao Tse-tung fought against opium. They would know that Ho Chi Minh fought against opium. The would know that Fidel Castro fought against drugs, and if they saw *Battle of Algiers* they would remember that the brothers in the NLF fought against drugs and killed the pusher. Fighting against drugs is revolutionary because drugs are a trick of the oppressor. The reason why drug use has reached the proportion it has today in our community is that the political consciousness of our people is rising, and in order to dull the political consciousness of our people, the oppressor sends more drugs into the community.

I have always felt that the highest criterion for a revolutionary is that he must have undying love for his people. To quote Che Guevara (and you should read him) : "At the risk of sounding romantic, a revolutionary must have a superhuman love for the masses of people." If one is concerned with one's people, one cannot see them committing genocide and stand idly by. People who are taking drugs are slowly committing genocide. If you care about them, you must speak out against the pushers of drugs in our community. We can clearly say to them, Look, man, we know you have to make a living somehow, we know because it's tough down here in this ghetto, a whole lot of funny things going on down here, but all of us have to walk tall. We can't be giving drugs to our people. A man has to walk tall. Now, you find another outlet for your drugs. You find another community for your drugs, but don't put it inside here, because you're killing our youth, and if you kill our youth, you kill our army, and if we don't have an army we can't fight and we're finished. And I believe in at least having a fighting chance.

To return to my second point, we must take over all these political institutions and that can be done through our politicians. Our politicians today have a great deal of power. The fact is that they have derived this power from the masses of our people. Especially since the slogan Black Power became popular. That's when all of them began to spring up. But they combine the concepts of Black Power with the frustrations of the masses and they use it to further themselves. This is opportunism. In our dialectic they are called "Black Power pimps." But you needn't worry about them, because if you know about revolution you would know that in the law of revolution they will be crushed. I have nothing to do with that. That is the law of revolution. The Bible says that in so many different ways, you know, whatever you sow, that you shall reap. Bible, not me. You don't have to worry about them, ain't too many more left anyhow.

They can't even sell themselves. They run to the white man: Yeah, I can do this, I can do that; white man doesn't even listen to them any more. There was a time when they could run up there and say to the white man, "There's been a rebellion in Chicago, there's been a rebellion in Watts, and if you don't give us some poverty money, there's going to be a rebellion in Washington," and the man gave them some money. But that's over now, because there have been rebellions all over. Not only that, but the white boy is prepared for rebellions today. He was buying time with his poverty program, because he wasn't prepared for rebellions. He wasn't prepared to deal with spontaneous rebellions in this black community. But he's prepared now. And since he's prepared now, our tactics must change. We've got to stay one step ahead of him. These political institutions can be taken over today through our politicians—by calling our politicians together and forcing them to unite and speak to our needs. We can begin to do so and I'll show you how later. But first, I want to repeat my ideology again and then follow with my tactics. Africa becomes our priority, number one. We seek for unity within our community, number two. We seek to take over the political institutions within our community, number three, and we seek to develop independent economic bases wherever possible, starting with our organizations. The police department must be taken over in our community. The judicial districts in our community must be taken over, and that can be done very easily. Then we'll say when a man commits a crime he will be tried in the area where he lives. Once you do that, you have automatically dismissed the question of a trial by the jury of one's peers. And of course, in our community, things will be different. Property damage will not mean as much. For us it will be human damage that will become the important thing. For example, if a brother raped a sister, he must get the death penalty immediately because he's touched a flower of the earth. He must get death because he has no respect for our women. In any ideology, while you're teaching and speaking to your ideology, you must have some sort of consequence if you disobey. That's what Christianity is about—if you don't do right you go to hell. That's what it boils down to, right? But since we are talking about an ideology that's secular, one that deals with the earth, if you commit a sin while you're here, you will pay for it while you're here.

We can rearrange our priorities once we have control of our judicial systems within our community. It can be done very easily. We can organize the black lawyers in our community to begin to speak to that. Many people say, Well, you can't get lawyers to do this and you can't get them to do that. That's true, but the reason is because we do not take time to organize. The black lawyers in our community have black clients, not white clients. Very few of them have white clients. If we pay the salary, we call the tune. That's how it is. They don't join the struggle, they don't have clients, simple as that. It calls, however, for organization. Many people are not willing to organize, they want to rap. They want to talk about how bad they are, but they're not willing to organize, and organization is our only solution. We must organize. We must take over the police stations in our community, because the honky policemen do not care about us. They're not here to protect us, they're only here to repress us. I want to tell you as a student of politics that the white policeman must withdraw from our community. They've got to go because we're peace-loving people and if they don't go I tell you as a student of politics that sniping against white policemen will escalate in our community. I am a student of politics. I studied politics well and I know it very, very well. I'm not here tonight to advocate violence or to advocate guerrilla warfare—that's a crime that can cause one's imprisonment and it is silly today for someone to go to jail for advocating guerrilla warfare. What I'm about to tell you is what is going to happen. Now, tomorrow I don't want you to go downtown and tell the man Carmichael said we should go get guns. No. No. Tell him Carmichael said "Given what is going down in this country, we are going to get guns."

Carmichael didn't say that you should go out and become guerrillas. Carmichael said "Given what is happening in the country, you are going to become guerrillas." Because I am giving an analysis, I am not encouraging guerrilla warfare. But while we are talking about guerrilla warfare, since I have been invited by the Institute of the Black World to lecture, and to lecture as a political scientist, and since in my area I have covered and done some academic work on guerrilla warfare, I would like to speak to you about guerrilla warfare largely on an academic level tonight.

I am not saying that you should go out and start sniping policemen, but I am saying that if they do not

212

withdraw from our community, sniping will escalate. We must understand how it will escalate. People have been discussing guerrilla warfare in this country. I would like, on an academic level, to explain how guerrilla warfare really works. You should take notes because you're students and you have to discuss these lectures. I mean you paid me to come here, you shouldn't sit there and waste your time, you should take notes—discuss it. If I'm right or if I'm wrong, discuss guerrilla warfare. A guerrilla never works in groups of more than three or five. Never. And the guerrilla never works with anybody he has not known for a long period of time. Any time you have thirteen people, or twenty-one people planning a conspiracy, that's not a guerrilla movement. You must remember the number one law of a guerrilla—the guerrilla's main supplier of arms is the enemy. That means when the guerrilla kills a member of the occupying army, he not only takes the gun that's around his waist, he opens up the door and he takes a 12-gauge shotgun. He opens up the trunk and takes all the ammunition, and he splits. Because the guerrilla must be victorious. And he buries the arms, in different places—only a little bit at a time. The guerrilla never stashes his arms at the office so that when the occupying army kick down the door they take all the guns. That makes no sense if one understands guerrilla warfare. The guerrilla hides his guns in areas here and there. The guerrilla knows how to break down the gun. He knows how to do it at night with his eyes closed. He can put together a gun and take it apart. He knows how to take care of guns, and the guerrilla never runs his mouth about how bad he is. That's a gorilla! Never! Never! But General Giap from North Vietnam quotes Mao that the guerrilla is like the fish in the sea. That is the theory. The guerrilla functions among the masses. It is from the masses that the guerrilla gets his support. Not only that, it's the masses that he hides among. If the masses are wearing dashikis, the guerrilla wears a dashiki. If the

213

masses are in church, the guerrilla is in church. Wherever the masses are, there the guerrilla is, and if you understand Christianity, you understand its real revolutionary message: "Wherever two or three are gathered, there I shall be also." The guerrilla never allows the enemy to provoke him into an attack before he is certain of victory. The guerrilla cannot afford defeat. He can only move when he is certain of victory. The masses are constantly watching the guerrilla, and if he is not victorious, they will not follow him. The guerrilla recruits from the masses. His goal is to make the masses guerrillas like himself. Therefore, as the guerrilla is more victorious, the masses will have more confidence in him. The enemy tries to make the guerrilla appear ridiculous in the eyes of the masses. He provokes the guerrilla, and if the guerrilla is stupid or miscalculates, he reacts to the provocation. Of course he dies a heroic death or is captured, but the masses will not follow him—only adventurers will. The masses want victory, not heroic deaths. We are all willing to die, but we want to know there is at least a *chance* of victory. If the guerrilla wants to move the masses, he must be organizing among the masses. There is one other thing that you must know about the guerrilla—the guerrilla studies. Now, if we'd all been doing that for fourteen months, we'd have a good nationwide organization in this country. We could have an above-ground political organization that will say, "We want the police stations." If the police stations are not delivered, a political consequence is dealt by the guerrilla. The guerrilla backs up the demands of the above-ground political organization. Again, I'm only speaking to you as an academician, merely as an academician, but I want to explain the theories to you.

The time of the guerrilla is limited, his time becomes very important. He can't waste time sitting up in an office jiving about revolution. If a guerrilla has a job, when he comes home from work, he studies, he studies. If you're talking about revolution, you had better get hip to studying. If you're not studying, you're doing nothing but fooling yourself. If you are a revolutionary today in the black community you must know Marx, you must know Lenin, you must know Malcolm X, Mao, Che, Fidel, Sékou Touré, Ho Chi Minh, you must know DuBois, you must know Nkrumah, you must know Lumumba, you must know Huey P. Newton, you must know LeRoi Jones, Robert Williams, you must know Fannie Lou Hamer, you must know a whole lot of people, a whole lot. Their ideas and their ideologies. Aside from that you must know what is going on in the world at the same time. You must understand the Warsaw pact and NATO, and what they represent. You must understand the internal contradictions of capitalism inside America. All these things are necessary if you are a true revolutionary. If you don't understand that, you're just running your mouth, because revolution is a science, and you've got to be scientific.

In a guerrilla movement you have an above-ground organization, and one below the ground—the military organization. The political organization makes the political demands. If they are not met, the guerrilla moves. No one knows who the guerrilla is. The guerrilla might be the same people in the political organization, for certainly the guerrilla must have a political ideology. You see, for example, all of us could come to a meeting. Let's say we call a meeting to decide we should have a police station here. All of you may be guerrillas, but we're not discussing guerrilla action. We make up our demands, and we go: "This is our demand, we want the police station, we want it in two weeks. You know? We want you to turn it over to our politicians. We want to be able to decide who our police captains are, because we want to clean up our community, and clearly the police are not doing it for us." And if the police station doesn't come to us in two weeks, maybe ten white policemen would be dead, their guns gone. In other words, the guerrilla deals a political consequence to the enemy. That's guerrilla warfare. The next time the political arm comes to speak, it has a real power base behind it, the community will begin to support the demands, and they will support the guerrilla actions if the demands are not met. You see, if you're talking about guerrilla warfare, you're talking about a highly organized community. You cannot have guerrilla warfare unless the community is thoroughly organized, and the community must be cleaned up. We cannot function in the community if we are afraid that if our sisters are out after twelve, or after eleven, or after dark, somebody might knock them in the head, take their pocketbook and run to buy some dope. We can't function if we're worried that some brother is trying to get us, we have to function free. For example, there are a lot of times the brothers may not be able to do something, so a sister's got to do it. You want to know that if a sister is running through the streets at two or three o'clock in the morning she has absolutely nothing to worry about. As a matter of fact, every brother is protecting her. Just for the functioning of guerrilla warfare, it is a necessity that we clean up and unite our community. We must do that.

I want to go back and talk about Ghana before I end. Lenin said that imperialism is the highest stage of capitalism. He is correct. Osagyefo, Dr. Kwame Nkrumah, says that neo-colonialism is the last stage of imperialism. He didn't say it was another stage. He didn't say it was the highest stage, he said it was the last stage of imperialism, and he's correct. We see that in neo-colonialist states in Africa, today. One of them is Ghana. The contradictions have arisen in Ghana. We see more and more the masses of people moving clearly forward to take that state. The people of Ghana are going to fight to take that state. They're going to crush the American-supported Busia regime into oblivion. That is written in the wind—the historical forces cannot be stopped. When they move to do that, my brothers and sisters, we must move to support them. If that state is taken, and

Osagyefo, Dr. Kwame Nkrumah, returns, we will have a land base that will be the first step towards the unification of our motherland and the first concrete victory of my ideology, which is Nkrumahism—the highest political expression of Pan-Africanism. I know you would not understand this because you haven't been allowed to read books by Kwame Nkrumah. There must be a reason for that. They called him a traitor, they called him a tyrant, they called him everything that is bad in the world, but Brother Malcolm X told you when they say something bad about a man then that's the man you should run to. The white boy seeks to destroy the leaders in our movement. And we are the people who are carried away with this nonsensical Western ideology: Oh, we don't need any leaders, we just need the right idea. Nonsense. A leader is the embodiment of the idea, it is he who carries that idea. Do you think that China would be China without Mao Tse-tung? Do you think Vietnam would be Vietnam without Ho Chi Minh? Do you think Cuba would be Cuba without Fidel Castro? Do you think England would be England without Churchill? Do you think France would be France without De Gaulle? Obviously not; a leader is the incorporation of ideas. Everybody knows this but us, we never protect our leaders until after they're dead; then we run to them. And the reason we do that is that we know once that leader has the correct ideology then nothing stands before us but the struggle or the open grave. But I will tell you that's right. I'm not going to tell you anything but the truth. The only thing I see before you is bloodshed, bloody, bloody bloodshed. But I'm going to tell you something else, that you can't run because they will try to kill you anyway, so you might as well prepare yourself for the fight. As Joe Louis says, "You can run but you can't hide."

I must tell you that the bloodshed that is coming for the Africans all over the world is a bloodshed that this world has never seen. Our struggle will be longer than the Vietnamese, our struggle will be more bloody than the Chinese Revolution, our struggle will be so bloody that sometime you will have to step over your brother while he is dead and keep running to hope you will avenge his death tomorrow. That's the bloodshed that lies before you. I do not lie to you. I do not promise you a quick victory. How can you say that in five years we're going to rip off the country? No, we have a generation of fight ahead of us, and whether you like it or not you had better prepare for it, because it's coming. If you think this white boy is not getting ready for a full genocide thing, you've got another thought coming. He does nothing but commit genocide against us. But I will also tell you with all the arrogance in the world that *we will win!*

We are going to win and it is already written in the wind. Check out the difference between us and the Jews when the Nazis started to commit genocide against them. They got the Jews to cooperate with them. They had Jews who were policemen; they had Jews who were on the governing board; they had Jews on all these boards, and the Jews were the ones who were carrying out the orders so the Nazis could say it's not us, it's the Jews and then they pulled the Uncle Tom Jews up. The reverse is beginning to happen in our communities. A month ago Roger Wilkins, a black man, even told them, "You can't use me against my people, if you think I am an Uncle Tom." He refused to serve on one of the Nixon committees.

We have to understand the processes of genocide so we'll understand precisely what they're doing. When the Germans got ready to commit genocide against the Jews, they weeded out all the generals from the army. Does it sound familiar? They're weeding them out here, even if you don't know it. You dig it? They started to isolate the Jewish community. They're doing it here, if you can dig it. It's a slower process, but they're doing it. They began to move to cut off all of the *assistances* to the Jewish communities. Check out your welfare cutoff, check it out.

218

We can play no more, play time is over. Ain't nothing out here but serious business. If you play you're going to get burned, so you might as well get serious and take a few with you. When they went in to get the Jews, the Jews didn't resist, until it was the last few of them left. But in our community, the reverse is true. They've tried to come into our community to get twenty-eight Black Panthers, the rank and file of the Panther Party, the most noble of our warriors. It cost them a bloody battle for the first twenty-eight, and instead of us becoming afraid, we become more arrogant when we drink of their blood, and become more determined. The next twenty-eight that they come to try and get, they're going to have to pay twice as high the price they paid for the first twenty-eight.

In closing, my brothers and sisters, during the past fourteen months, I have been to Egypt, Tanzania, Nigeria, Congo Brazzaville, Sierra Leone, Senegal, the Sudan, and, of course, I live under the progressive leadership of the great President Ahmed Sékou Touré in Guinea. I have spoken to people all over Africa. I have spoken at youth rallies, I have spoken at universities, I have spoken with government officials, and in these circles the support for Osagyefo, Dr. Kwame Nkrumah, is growing by leaps and bounds! My wife and I visited in Nigeria in February and I had the opportunity to speak at the University of Ibadan, the same university, incidentally, that Brother Malcolm X spoke at. I had the greatest pleasure of my life when I spoke on the very same platform that Brother Malcolm spoke on in Nigeria.

When Osagyefo was overthrown in 1965, the Nigerian press said, Good, the tyrant is gone, the traitor is finished, it's all over. The dictator of Africa, the man who wanted Africa for himself, is gone. Can you dig this! They said the man who wanted Africa for himself is finished. The white boy drew up boundaries and gave them Nigeria, they were content with Nigeria. I want the steak, I don't want the crumbs. If the meat belongs to me I'm going to have it or nobody is going to get it. That's the way I work. I don't want crumbs, I won't fight for crumbs, I'm fighting for the steak. My life is on the line, so I'm going for broke. I won't go through that, if I take one step, get a little piece, take another—no, it belongs to me. Keep your hands off of it, it's mine. That's right. And until I get it, I'm going to keep trying to get it. If all I'm doing is sitting in a corner and watching you, don't think I've forgot, I'm scheming my brains off to get it. Dig it? You see me lying down in the corner don't say, Oh, he's finished. I'm not finished, I'm scheming for the best way to get it, and the quickest way to get it too. Ghana is going to be taken by the masses of Ghanaians. Osagyefo will return to Ghana, and we must support that movement.

Keep on fighting, they can't wipe us out. They have killed a lot of us and they will kill a lot more. But we will study, organize, and prepare, and we will win—we will destroy them as sure as the night follows day! For in the final analysis, revolution is always about the truth and justice—that which is just. And of all the people on the face of this earth, we are the most just.

15

From
Black Power
Back to
Pan-
Africanism

Pan-Africanism is grounded in the belief that Africa is one; the artificial borders being the result of the Berlin conference, where European powers carved up the continent and divided the spoils among themselves. Pan-Africanism is grounded in the belief that all African peoples, wherever we may be, are one, and as Dr. Nkrumah says, "belong to the African nation"; our dispersal was the result of European imperialism and racism. Pan-Africanism is grounded in socialism which has its roots in communalism. Any ideology seeking to solve the problems of the African people must find its roots in Pan-Africanism.

Problems must be posed correctly. All the components

must be put together and viewed as a whole. The historical conditions must be seen in correct perspective. Pan-Africanists study the history of Africa and her people. African history is rarely recorded as the history of Africans; it is usually reported as an offshoot of European history. Consequently, when we have studied our history the starting point has usually been the "discovery" of the African by the European. Thus our brothers and sisters in the Western Hemisphere begin our history with slavery, and on the continent we begin with colonialism, and these two facts are not joined. This incorrect analysis makes for incorrect solutions. Africans in the Western Hemisphere view part of the problem (slavery) as an entity. On the continent another part (colonialism) is seen as an unrelated entity. The problem is compounded on the continent by the fact that each country is isolated as a separate entity. Algerians see their problems as the plight of Algerians, Kenyans as Kenyans, South Africans as South Africans, etc., etc. This parochial thinking must cease. Our starting point in history must precede the period of colonialism and slavery; it must precede the Arabic and European invasions. This is not to say we want to rest on the past glory of African civilization, which contributed immensely to world civilization; but in order to map out the future we *must* clearly understand the past. More importantly, this interpretation allows us to view the effects these events had on us. Thus we are reminded in *Consciencism** that our history must be seen as a whole, as "the history of *our* society."

Africans today, irrespective of geographical location, have a common enemy and face common problems. We are the victims of imperialism, racism, and we are a landless people. That we are the victims of imperialism is a fact. That we are the victims of racism is crystal clear; the epitome of this brutal form of oppression finds its or-

* By Dr. Kwame Nkrumah.

ganized political expression in South Africa, the Portuguese colonies, and of course the United States of America. We should not forget South America, Brazil in particular, where a sizable proportion of the population are Africans, who suffer racial discrimination. On the question of landlessness the African is divided into two groups. One group was taken from the land (slavery), the second group had the land taken from them (colonialism). These facts all point toward the need for a combined effort to solve our common problems, thus Pan-Africanism.

The concept of Pan-Africanism is not new. It found its expression in African revolts during slavery, and reached its organizational level in the early part of the twentieth century. From then until now, some aspects of Pan-Africanism have been found in every movement that sought to liberate Africans. If we interpret our history correctly, we will note that these movements, seemingly unrelated, were either consciously or subconsciously moving in a concerted effort towards Pan-Africanism. The movement had its high and low points, but it has never been dissipated. All the intellectual giants of the African world have been baptized in Pan-Africanism. Although Pan-Africanism has its origin among the Africans of the diaspora, Mother Africa is its *sine qua non*. Africans on both sides of the Atlantic contributed immensely to the ideology, but only in Africa will we see its fruition. Dr. W. E. Burghardt Du Bois, Mr. Henry Sylvester-Williams, Attorney Joseph Casely-Hayford, Attorney Ladipo Solanke, Mr. George Padmore, the Honorable Marcus Garvey, Patrice Lumumba, Malcolm X, Ben Bella, President Ahmed Sékou Touré and President Kwame Nkrumah are a few of the giants. All of these great men saw and still see the unity of Africans as the indisputable prerequisite for complete liberation. They were and are Pan-Africanists in thought, word, and deed. They are all Africans. They saw and felt the oppression of their people and pledged their lives to end that suffering. Their dream was and is to restore dignity to Mother Africa and her children. They are victims of racism; it is only natural they should be anti-racist. They are also anti-imperialist. They contend that capitalism is an alien system in Africa and all traces must be destroyed.

Unfortunately in this essay we can not discuss the history and development of Pan-Africanism. That task was undertaken by Mr. Vincent Bakpetu Thompson in his excellent book *Africa and Unity: The Evolution of Pan-Africanism*. At certain periods of our history Pan-Africanism faced what appeared to be insurmountable obstacles. At the first Pan-African congress, practically all of Africa was colonized. Thus Pan-Africanism remained on the level of theories and protestations. Today, even with nominal independence on our continent, Pan-Africanism finds fertile ground. When Casely-Hayford was calling out to his brothers across the Atlantic, Ghana was the "Gold Coast" and Britain her master. When Kwame Nkrumah stretched out his hands to his brothers, Ghana was independent and Nkrumah her leader. When Marcus Garvey said that unless Africa is free, Africans the world over would not be free, he was answered by a counter-revolutionary President King of Liberia who wanted no relations with his brothers. But Brother Malcolm X addressed the Organization of African Unity. Marcus Garvey never set foot on Africa, and Brother Malcolm was treated like a shining African prince. Africans of the diaspora have been moving at a rapid pace towards Pan-Africanism, but very few people have analyzed that movement correctly. Brother Malcolm told us we needed Black Nationalism. But Black Nationalism is African Nationalism. Because the Blackman is the African and the African is the Blackman. Thus Brother Malcolm's Black Nationalism is really African Nationalism. African Nationalism finds its highest aspiration in Pan-Africanism. So too Black Power really means African Power. The African's power base is his homeland—Mother Africa. In order to achieve African power, Mother Africa must be strong. To be strong she must be unified. Modern-day Pan-Africanism, which finds its highest political expression in Nkrumahism, holds as its basic tenet "the total liberation and unification of Africa under an All-African socialist government." As soon as this goal is achieved, Africans the world over will not only be respected but will have the Black Power to demand respect. This must be our primary objective and it must be relentlessly pursued, no matter what the sacrifice. It is a prerequisite for world peace.

It is usual procedure for advocates of Pan-Africanism to assure Africans of the diaspora that Pan-Africanism does not mean returning to Africa. I refuse to do so. In the past I have fallen victim to this chronic ailment of inferiority complex. We are Africans. Africa is our home. Even if a man cannot return home it is his dying wish. Africa is the richest and most beautiful continent in the world. Our continent is plunged in exploitation and oppression, both external and internal; the internal oppressors receiving their lifeblood from Africa's external enemies. The suffering of Africa is beyond description. Those suffering from chronic inferiority complexes observe the continent superficially and conclude that Africa is fated for eternal doom. Pan-Africanists know better. Mother Africa is ours, we are proud of her and to her glorious reconstruction we pledge our lives.

The question now facing us is how best to achieve our objective. In order to launch a clear program, we must have land bases. We must have countries with leaders like President Nkrumah and President Touré willing to surrender their sovereignty to a larger African community. For our purposes, we can divide Africa's states into three groups: (a) progressive states, (b) neocolonialist states and (c) European settler colonies. At this time we must consolidate our power. Therefore we must support the peoples and governments of those too-few progressive states. These leaders whose only surplus is scarcity are fighting against overwhelming odds to bring their states into true scientific socialism. Not the least among these odds is the refusal of the Uncle Tom leaders to unite on programs for the good of Africa. Neocolonialist states can be divided into two groups: states that went directly from colonialism to neocolonialism, and states that passed through the stage of genuine political independence. We must concentrate on these latter states, where the leaders had an opportunity to educate the masses, thus laying the foundation for real socialism. After coups d'etat and assassinations, these states were returned to neocolonialism with the aid of African traitors. These states in the very near future will reach the Dialectical Moment when, given the correct objective conditions, two diametrically opposed philosophies will clash. Of these states Ghana is the most important because of the work of Osagyefo, who had developed Ghana into the center of Pan-African activity for the world. By overthrowing Dr. Nkrumah the enemies and traitors of the African people sought to destroy Pan-Africanism. But it has had the reverse effect. Pan-Africanists now have unity of purpose. Pan-Africanism has crystallized around Ghana's tragic descent into neocolonialism, and Pan-Africanists of the world have cast their lot with the suffering masses of Ghana. Among them stand such African leaders and people as the great Ahmed Sékou Touré and our brothers and sisters of Guinea. The battle lines are drawn. We stand with the masses against African traitors who serve as puppets. In the European settler colonies which contaminate our continent and people, we must prepare for protracted struggle and a fight to the death. No amount of talk, appeals to conscience or even appeals to world organizations will solve that problem. The only solution is to drive these disrupters of our society into the sea. We can expect and should accept the fact that European powers will fight with the settlers; after all they are "kith and kin" and they fight to protect their own interests. The fight against the settlers is doomed to failure if it is not an All-African fight. Our brothers and sisters in these colonies are incapable of achieving victory alone, because they are fighting NATO.* Even if they could achieve victory alone we must help them, because every square inch of Africa belongs to all of us. To view the settler colonies as separate entities is to miss the boat. In order to remove the contamination from our continent, we must unite all our available resources. Seen in this light, the neocolonialist states are crucial. These states must swing the pendulum. Once liberated from the tentacles of imperialism, and united with the progressive states, they will yield a stronger revolutionary base from which to launch our attacks against the enemies of Mother Africa and her people.

The African for the last five hundred years has known neither peace nor justice. His wealth and his labor have built Western Europe and America. When these forces are harnessed for our benefit, the reconstruction of Mother Africa will be worthy of her glorious past. The setback in Ghana is no cause for dismay. Pan-Africanists know that setbacks are not new to the African struggle; this one has not even been long. We are not afraid of the inevitable bloodshed, for beyond it we see victory in the air.

* North Atlantic Treaty Organization (United States and Western European military establishment).